World's Greatest
ENTERTAINERS

Wonder House

(An imprint of Prakash Books)

Wonder House

(An imprint of Prakash Books)

contact@wonderhousebooks.com

ISBN : 9789388810357

CONTENTS

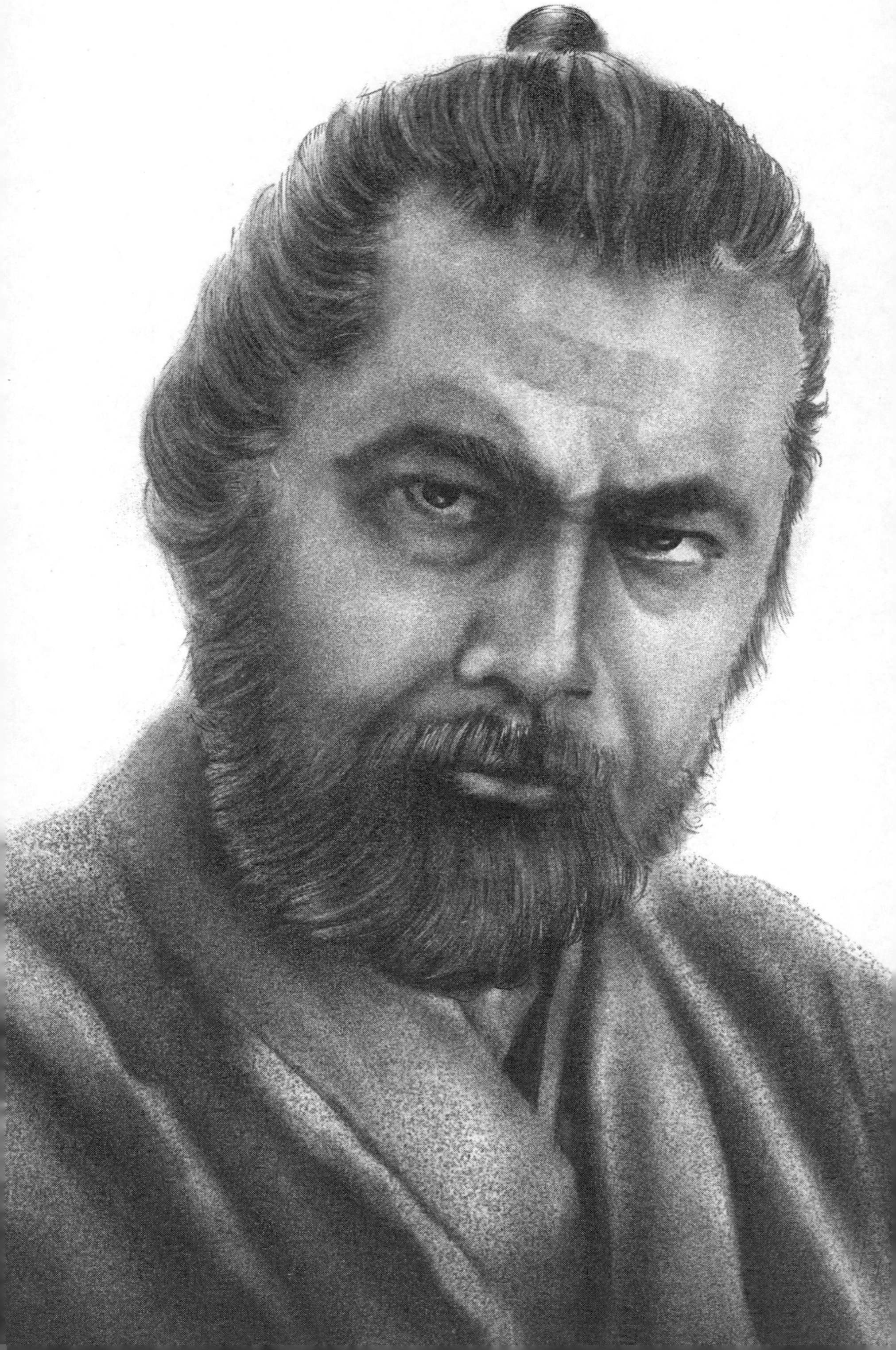

AKIRA KUROSAWA

BIRTH: March 23, 1910
Shinagawa, Tokyo, Japan

DEATH: September 6, 1998 (aged 88)
Setagaya, Tokyo, Japan

Akira Kurosawa was a Japanese film director and screenwriter. He introduced Japanese cinema in the Western market and became the first Japanese director to gain international acclaim.

Akira Kurosawa was born on March 23, 1910

in Tokyo. His father, Isamu, an army officer who later became a physical education teacher. His mother, Shima Kurosawa, was a homemaker.

Kurosawa attended art school after his secondary education. He began to paint in the Western style. He also learned Calligraphy and Kendo swordsmanship and won many art prizes. His elder brother, Heigo, was a narrator for silent films. Heigo committed suicide in 1933, which deeply affected the then 23-year old Kurosawa.

Kurosawa began as an assistant director at Photo Chemical Laboratories (PCL Studios; later known as Toho Films) in 1936 under Yamamoto Kajiro's supervision. In 1943, he directed his first film, *Sanshiro Sugata*, about Japanese judo masters. It gained much critical and commercial acclaim.

In 1944, he released *Ichiban Utsukushiku (The Most Beautiful)*, which featured hardworking female factory workers. His film *Yoidore Tenshi (Drunken Angel)* was chosen as the 'Best Film of the Year' by the Kinema Junpo critics.

Kurosawa's *Rashomon* was released in 1950. It was based on a thrilling short story about a samurai's murder. *Rashomon* received much international recognition and praise. It won the Academy Award for 'Best Foreign Film' and was also appreciated at the Venice Film Festival. His *Shinchinin No Samurai (Seven Samurai),* a three-and-a-half-hour epic movie, is considered to be some of his best work.

Kurosawa released *Throne of Blood,* an adaptation of Shakespeare's *Macbeth*, in 1957. The next year, he released *Hidden Fortress,* which was his first film in the wide-screen format.

He set up Kurosawa Productions in 1960, and became its president. He made many entertaining films including *Yojimbo (The Bodyguard)* and *Akahige (Red Beard).* He started shooting for his first Hollywood film *Tora! Tora! Tora!* in 1968 for 20th Century Fox, at the Kyōto studio. But later on, Kurosawa was replaced with another director due to financial issues.

In 1975, Kurosawa filmed *Dersu Uzala* in Siberia, at the invitation of the Soviet government. The storyline follows the life of a Siberian hermit. It won him many awards and honors, including the Academy Award for 'Best Foreign Language Film'. In 1980, Kurosawa's *Kagemusha (The Shadow Warrior)* was released. It received the Palm d'Or at Cannes, a British Academy of Film and Television Arts (BAFTA) Award, and a Cesar Award, and was also nominated at the Academy Awards in the 'Best Foreign Film' category. His next film *Ran (The Chaos)*, an adaptation of Shakespeare's *King Lear*, was even more successful.

The last film directed by Kurosawa was *Madadayo (Not Ready Yet)*. He was working on a project in 1995 when he fell and broke his spine. He had to start using a wheelchair after this incident.

Kurosawa was awarded the Golden Prize and Prix FIPRESCI at the Moscow International Film Festival for his brilliant work as a director.

He was also honored with an Academy

Honorary Award by the Academy of Motion Picture Arts and Science in 1990. This award was presented to him by George Lucas and Steven Spielberg. He was named 'Asian of the Century' by the *AsianWeek* magazine. Many of his films have been adapted by English filmmakers. His Rashomon was adapted as *The Outrage* in 1964, starring William Shatner, and *The Magnificent Seven*, directed by John Sturges, is based on Kurosawa's *Seven Samurai*.

Kurosawa married the actress Yoko Yaguchi in 1945. They had two children together. Kurosawa passed away on 6th September, 1998 due to a stroke.

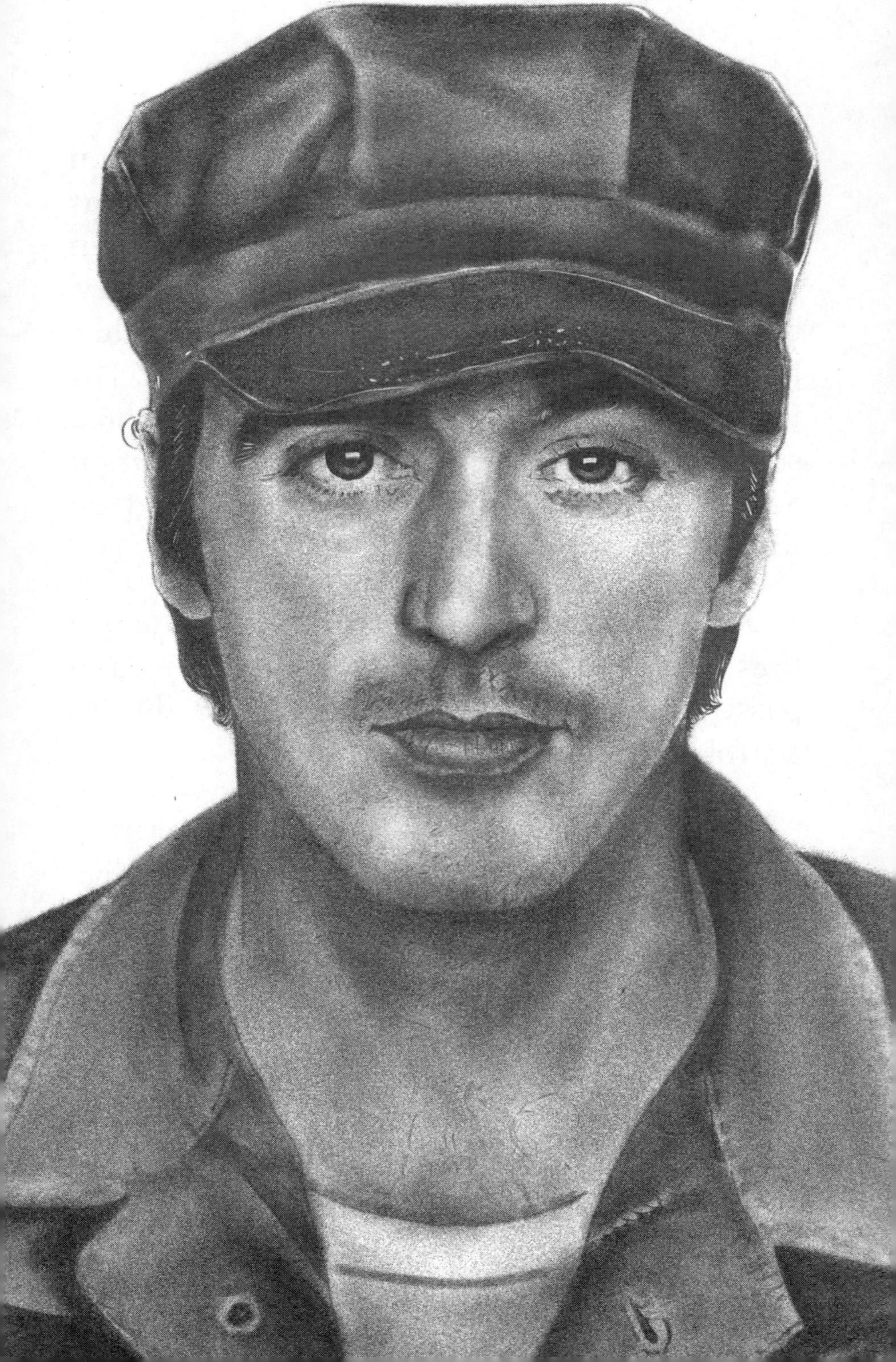

AL PACINO

BIRTH: *April 25, 1940*
East Harlem, New York, USA

Al Pacino is an American actor and director. He is known for his legendary roles in *The Godfather, Serpico* and *Scent of a Woman.*

Alfredo James Pacino was born on April 25, 1940 in New York, to Rose and Salvatore Pacino. His parents separated when he was two years old. His mother and grandparents raised him in Bronx. Al's interest in acting developed at an early age. Al Pacino found his classes boring but found a haven in school plays. He kept repeating dialogs from movies.

In the initial days he went through a period of financial instability, where he had to borrow money even for his bus fare. In 1959, he moved to Greenwich to pursue a career in acting. He studied acting at the Herbert Berghof Studio (HBO Studio). He became close friends with his acting teacher, Charlie Laughton.

After performing supporting roles in many plays, Pacino started getting bigger acting roles in off-broadway productions. In 1963, he played a role in William Saroyan's play *Hello, Out There*. He got accepted to the prestigious Actors Studio in 1966 and studied under Lee Strasberg. He was part of the Broadway production *Does the Tiger Wear a Necktie?* He received a Tony Award for his performance. Pacino also played a minor role in the movie, *Me, Natalie* in 1969.

He played the role of Bobby in *The Panic in Needle Park* in 1971. But, Pacino is most known for his performance in Francis Ford Coppola's *The Godfather*. It was based on a novel of the same name written by Mario Puzo. Pacino played the character of Michael Corleone. It is considered to be one of the greatest films of all time. This role earned him an Academy Award nomination in the 'Supporting Actor' category.

Pacino acted in *Serpico* in 1973, a movie based on a true story about a policeman in New York City. He reappeared as Michael Corleone in *The Godfather: Part II*. He starred in the 1975 film *Dog Day Afternoon*, playing the role of Sonny Wortzik. This role landed him another Academy Award nomination .

His movies from the 1980s include *Scarface, Cruising, Author! Author!* and *Revolution*. He also performed theater during this time. He appeared in David Mamet's play, *American Buffalo* and played Marc Antony in *Julius Caesar* in a New York Shakespeare Festival production. In 1989, he was part of the thriller movie, *Sea of Love*.

Pacino rejoined the cast for *The Godfather: Part III* in 1990, for which he was nominated for an Academy Award in the 'Best Actor' category .

In the 1990s, he acted in movies like *Frankie and Johnny, Scent of a Woman, Donnie Brasco, The Devil's Advocate* and *Insider*. He wrote, directed and performed for the documentary *Looking for Richard*. It is an exploration of Shakespeare's *Richard III*.

Pacino acted in and directed *Chinese Coffee* in 1999. He also played a part in its Broadway version. In 2007, he appeared in *Oceans' Thirteen* alongside stars like George Clooney and Matt Damon. Pacino had a role in the TV movie *You Don't Know Jack*. It received much critical appreciation. Pacino directed *Wilde Salome* in 2011. It was based on the life of Oscar Wilde.

Pacino has received eight Academy Award nominations so far. He won one for *Scent of a Woman*. His role in the *Godfather* series is recognized as the eleventh most iconic villain in film history by the American Film Institute. He has also won four Golden Globes and has been awarded two Tony Awards for his performance on stage.

Pacino received the Golden Globe Cecil B. DeMille Award in 2001. He was voted the greatest film star of all time by British television viewers in 2003. In 2007, he was honored with the Lifetime Achievement Award by the American Film Institute. He was honored with the National Medal of Arts in 2011. In 2016, he was bestowed with the Kennedy Center Honors.

Pacino was a part of the 2001 benefit concert 'America: A Tribute to Heroes' to raise funds for the victims of 9/11.

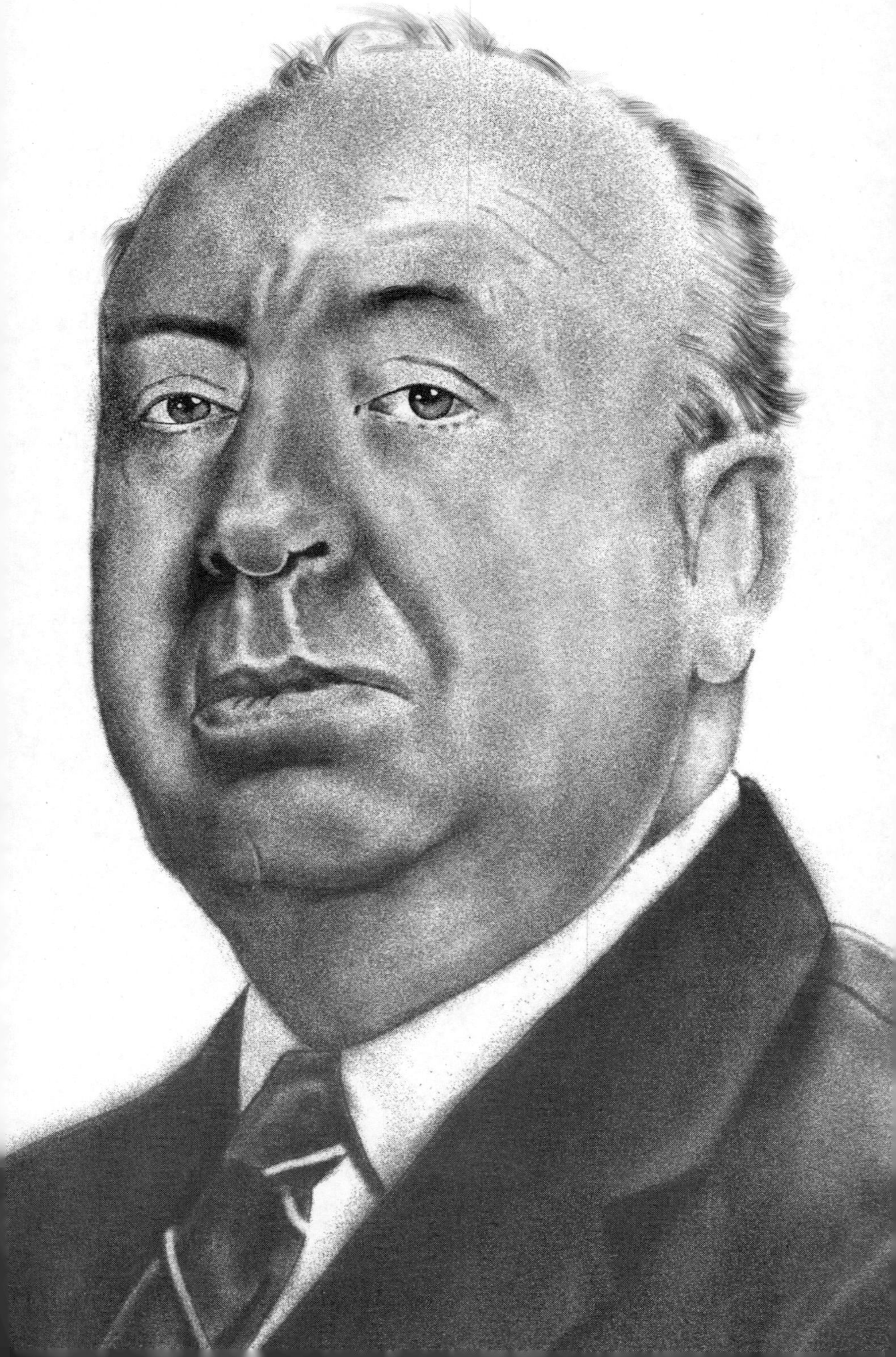

ALFRED HITCHCOCK

BIRTH: August 13, 1899
Leytonstone, Essex, England

DEATH: April 29, 1980 (aged 80)
Bel Air, California, USA

Alfred Hitchcock was an English film director, producer and screenwriter. He is famously referred to as the 'Master of Suspense' for creating intense psychological suspense films. He directed 53 films in a career of 51 years. *Rear Window, North by Northwest, Vertigo* and *Psycho* are considered to be his best movies.

Alfred Hitchcock was born on August 13, 1899,

in London, England to William Hitchcock and Emma Jane Hitchcock. He was raised in a strict Catholic family.

Hitchcock's first job was as an advertising designer at W.T. Henley's Telegraph Works Company. This company had an in-house publication called *The Henley Telegraph*. He also showed an interest in photography and film production.

Hitchcock was then employed as a title card designer at the Famous Players-Lasky Company in Islington in 1920. As a director, Hitchcock started directing his first film *Mrs. Peaboy*, but the film couldn't be completed because of financial issues. Later in 1923, he released his first film, *Always Tell Your Wife*, co-directed with Seymour Hicks. In 1925, Hitchcock made his solo directorial debut in *The Pleasure Garden*.

Hitchcock's *The Lodger: A Story of the London Fog* was released in 1927. It was based on a series of murders in London, where a man is accused of being a Jack-the-ripper like killer. It gained both commercial and critical acclaim. Hitchcock's

Blackmail was his first talking film. Two of his thrillers from the 1930s, *The Lady Vanishes* and *The 39 Steps* were ranked in a list of the greatest British films of the twentieth century. The movement of the camera and his direction style came to be referred to as "Hitchcockian".

Hitchcock was approached by David O. Selznick to create movies for Hollywood. Before moving to California, he made one last movie in England in 1939, it was called *Jamaica Inn*. His family then moved to California, where he continued to create his masterpieces.

His 1940 release, *Rebecca*, won the Academy Award for 'Best Picture'. The American studios provided him with a greater variety of devices to be employed for production. The suspense thrillers he created in Hollywood included *Notorious, Strangers on a Train, Rear Window, Vertigo* and *Psycho.*

His complex characters, coupled with a characteristic depiction of violence, began to represent his style in cinema. *Alfred Hitchcock Presents* was a television series that aired from

1955-1962 on CBS and NBC. It was hosted and produced by Hitchcock, and explored the main elements that dominated his works. It was recognized as one of 'The 100 Best TV Shows of All Time' by *Time* magazine.

The master of suspense was inducted to the Hollywood Walk of Fame in 1960. He has been awarded two Golden Globe awards. He was also honored with a BAFTA Fellowship. Hitchcock has been nominated for an Academy Award five times. He won one in 1968 in the 'Best Picture' category.

Hitchcock was honored with the American Film Institute (AFI) Lifetime Achievement Award in 1979. He was soon also knighted. In 2012, the British Film Institute declared *Vertigo* as the greatest film ever made.

Hitchcock married Alma Reville in 1926. His wife worked as an assistant director and collaborator in his films. Their daughter, Patricia Hitchcock, was born in 1928. She has acted in Hitchcock's films, *Psycho* and *Strangers on a Train*.

Alfred Hitchcock passed away in his sleep on April 29, 1980, in California. The cause of his death was kidney failure. His remains were scattered in the Pacific Ocean.

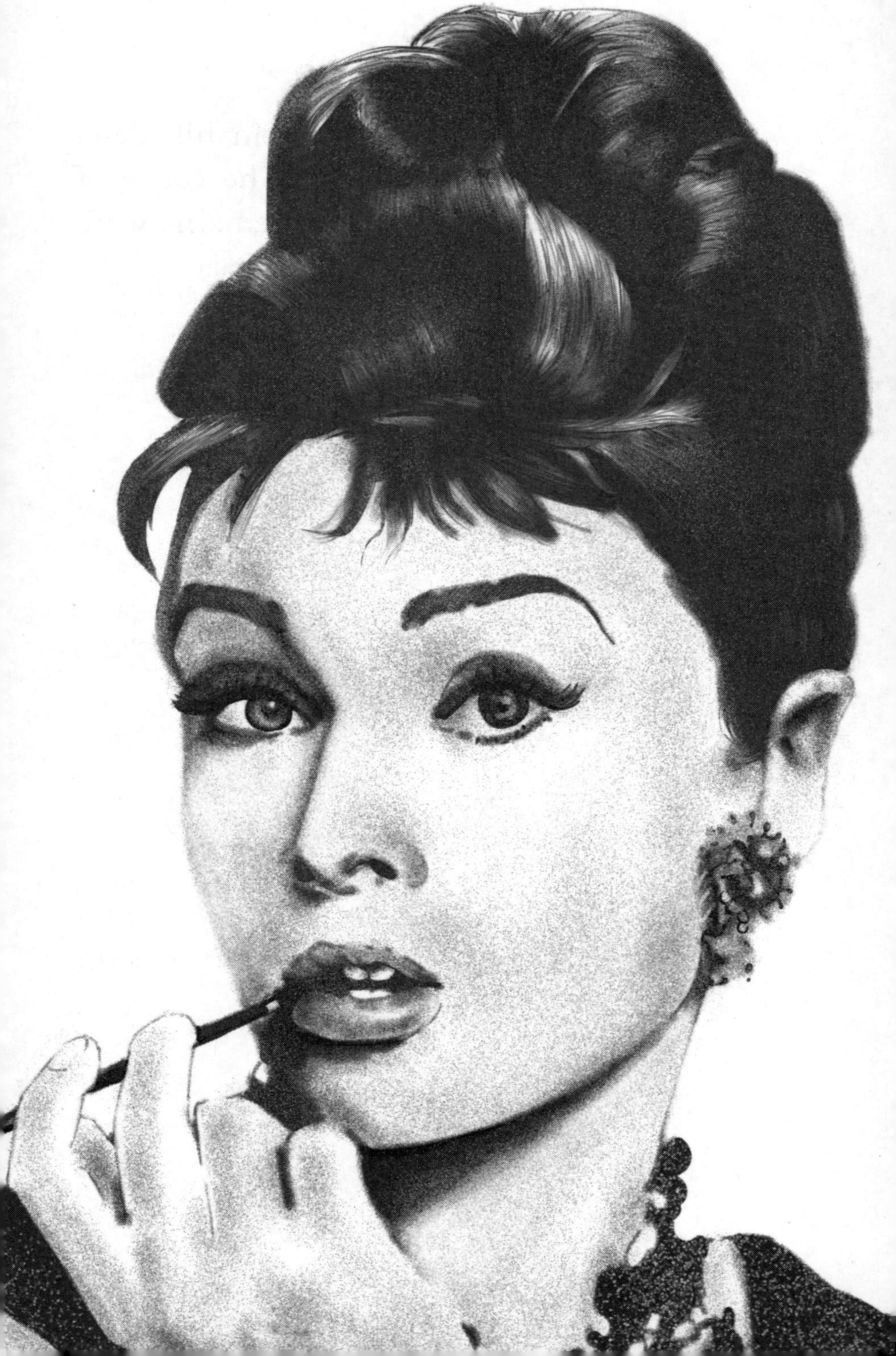

AUDREY HEPBURN

BIRTH: *May 4, 1929*
Ixelles, Brussels, Belgium

DEATH: *January 20, 1993 (aged 63)*
Tolochenaz, Vaud, Switzerland

Audrey Hepburn was a British actress, dancer and model. She is best known for her iconic role in *Breakfast at Tiffany's*. She is still considered to be the greatest style icon in Hollywood.

Hepburn was born in Brussels, Belgium on May 4, 1929. She was born to Joseph Victor Anthony Ruston and Ella Van Heemstra.

Her parents separated when she was a child. She studied at a boarding school in England. She attended the Arnhem Conservatory in the Netherlands during the Second World War, and received ballet training in Amsterdam and London. She made her stage debut in the chorus of *Sauce Tartare.* The next year she featured as a player in *Sauce Piquante.*

Hepburn made her debut with the feature film *One Wild Oat* in 1951. It was soon followed by *Young Wives Tales* and *The Lavender Hill Mob.* Hepburn bagged a lead role in the play *Gigi* in 1951, which gained her much recognition.

She acted as a ballet dancer in *The Secret People* in 1952. In 1953, she played one of her most celebrated roles, Princess Anne, in the movie *Roman Holiday.* She received an Academy Award for 'Best Actress' for her performance. In 1954, she was part of the Broadway production of *Ondine* opposite Mel Ferrer. She received a Tony Award for this role. This was followed by the romantic comedy *Sabrina,* for which she received an Academy Award nomination.

Hepburn exuded glamour and style playing the character of Holly Golightly in the 1961 classic, *Breakfast at Tiffany's*. It was based on a novella by Truman Capote. Hepburn considered it to be her most challenging role because the character of the socialite differed from her personality tremendously. This role got her another nomination at the Academy Awards.

Hepburn starred opposite Cary Grant in *Charade* in 1963. She played Eliza Doolittle in the film adaptation of the musical *My Fair Lady*. She acted opposite Alan Arkin in the suspense film *Wait Until Dark,* which earned her immense critical acclaim and another nomination at the Academy Awards.

Hepburn worked with Sean Connery in the Robin Hood saga *Robin and Marian.* She was also a part of the thriller *Bloodline* with Ben Gazzara, which was based on a Sidney Sheldon novel. In 1981, Hepburn and Gazzara worked together again in *They All Laughed.* She last acted in Steven Spielberg's romantic-comedy *Always,* in 1989.

Hepburn was named 'Promising Personality of 1951-52' by the Theatre World Awards. In 1952, she was awarded the Billboard Annual Donaldson Award. She received an Academy Award for 'Best Actress', a Golden Globe, and a BAFTA, all for *Roman Holiday*. She was also honored with a Tony Award in the category of 'Best Dramatic Actress' for her performance in *Ondine*.

Hepburn was inducted to the Hollywood Walk of Fame in 1960. She also received the NYFCC Best Actress Award in the same year. In 1992, she was awarded the BAFTA Lifetime Achievement Award.

In the late 1980s, Hepburn was an ambassador for UNICEF. In 1993, she received an Academy Award for her humanitarian work. She was also honored with the Presidential Medal of Freedom. In 2002, a statue of Hepburn was placed at the headquarters of UNICEF called 'The Spirit of Audrey'. Her sons established the Audrey Hepburn Society at the US Fund for UNICEF.

Hepburn married her co-star Mel Ferrer in 1954. They had a son together and divorced after fourteen years of marriage. In 1969, she married the psychiatrist, Andrea Dotti. They also had a son, but got divorced in 1982. She passed away on January 20, 1993 due to appendicular cancer.

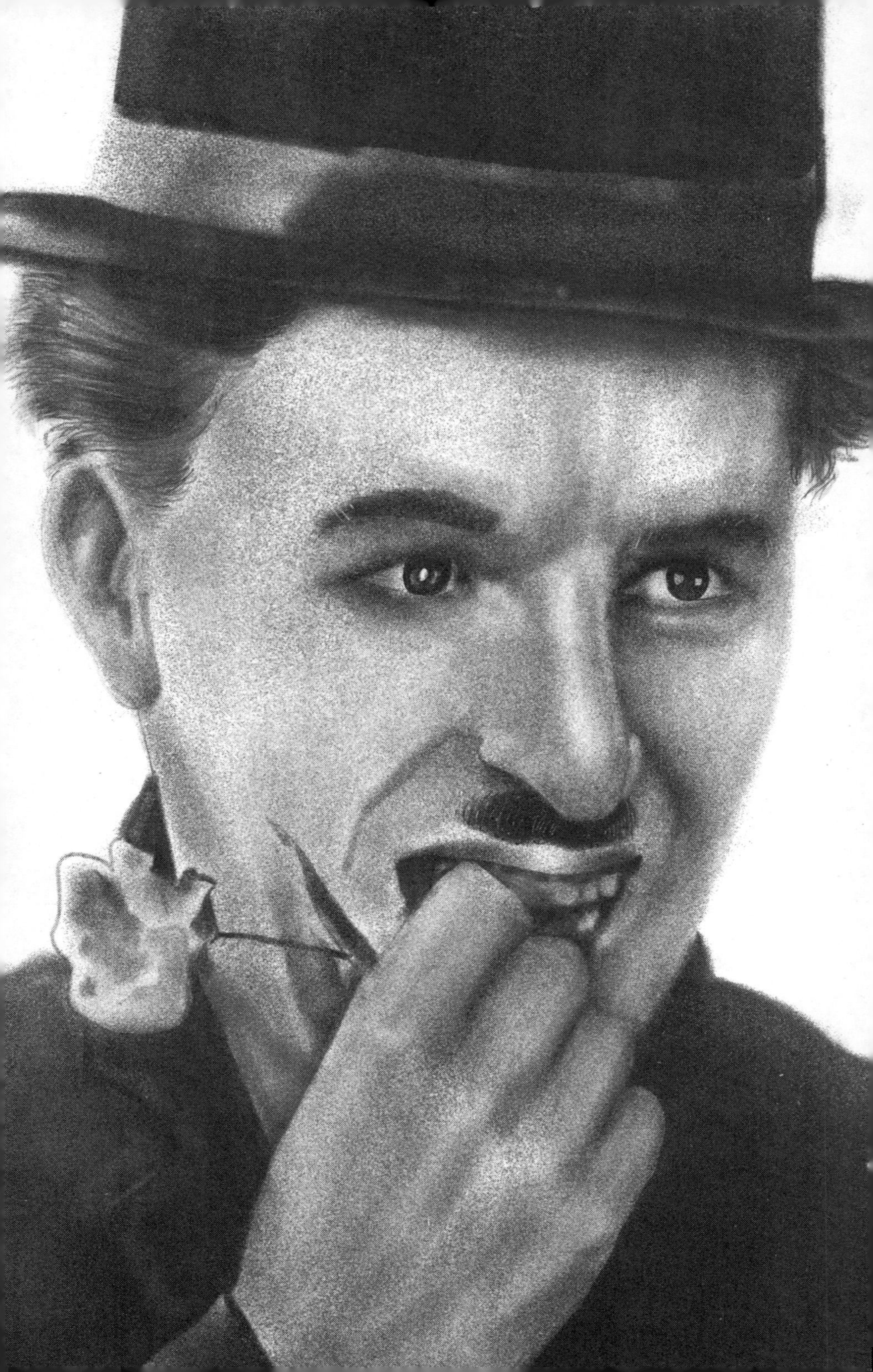

CHARLIE CHAPLIN

BIRTH: *April 16, 1889, England*

DEATH: *December 25, 1977 (aged 88)*
Corsier-sur-Vevey, Vaud, Switzerland

Sir Charles Spencer Chaplin was an English actor and director. He is regarded as one of the most iconic figures in the history of cinema. His famous performances include *The Kid, The Great Dictator* and *The Immigrant.*

Chaplin was born on April 16, 1889 in England. His parents, Hannah Chaplin and Charles Chaplin, Sr. were music hall entertainers. He faced penury in his childhood.

Chaplin was part of a male dance troupe called The Eight Lancashire Lads, from 1898 to 1900. They toured the music halls of Britain. In 1903, he acted as a newsboy in Jim, a *Romance of Cockayne.* He became a member of the comedy troupe Casey's Court Circus in 1906.

Chaplin finally bagged a lead role in the sketch *Jimmy the Fearless,* in 1910. He gained much recognition and popularity after this project. He signed a contract with the New York Motion Picture Company in 1913. He made his debut in the feature film *Making a Living* in 1914.

Chaplin first appeared in his most memorable role as the Little Tramp in *Kid Auto Races at Venice* in 1914. He was part of several movies by Keystone Studios such as, *Between Showers, A Film Johnnie* and *His Favorite Pastime.* Chaplin had acted in over thirty movies by the following year.

In 1915, Chaplin directed and wrote movies for Essanay Film Manufacturing Company, like *The Tramp.* It is considered to be Chaplin's first classic. Other classics of his include, *A Night Out, A Woman, Police* and *The Bank.*

Chaplin shifted to Mutual Film Corporation in 1916. He wrote, directed, produced and acted in their films. The movies from his time there are *The Rink, The Vagabond, The Count* and *Easy Street.* From 1918 to 1923, his movies were distributed by the First National Exhibitors' Circuit. Chaplin co-founded United Artists Corporation in 1919 with D. W. Griffith, Mary Pickford and Douglas Fairbanks.

Chaplin acted in, directed and produced *The Gold Rush* in 1925. It earned an Academy Award. His film *Circus* was released in 1928. He played the role of a clown in this seventy-minute-long silent film. It became his highest grossing silent film.

In 1936, his film *Modern Times* was released. It reflected on the struggles of living in an industrial world in a satirical manner. Chaplin next portrayed the role of a Jewish barber in *The Great Dictator.* This movie parodied the German dictator Adolf Hitler.

Chaplin directed and acted in the comedy *A King in New York* (1957), once again dabbling in creating a satirical portrayal of the social and political situation in the United States of America. His last movie was *A Countess from Hong Kong,* released in 1967.

Chaplin was awarded the Honorary Academy Award in 1929, and again in 1972. He was also inducted to the Hollywood Walk of Fame in 1972. He received an Academy Award for 'Best Music, Original Dramatic Score' for *Limelight.*

His movie *Modern Times* ranked 33rd in the American Film Institute's '100 funniest movies in America'. *The Gold Rush* was ranked as the second greatest film in history by the Brussels World's Fair.

Charlie Chaplin was married four times. His last marriage was to Oona O'Neill. Chaplin was a father to eleven children. He passed away on December 25, 1977, at the age of 88, due to a stroke. Chaplin was interred at Vevey cemetery in Switzerland.

In 2010, 'Charlie Chaplin—The Great Londoner', an exhibition on Chaplin's life opened at the London Film Museum. He was included in *Time* magazine's list of '100 Most Important People of the 20th Century' in 1998.

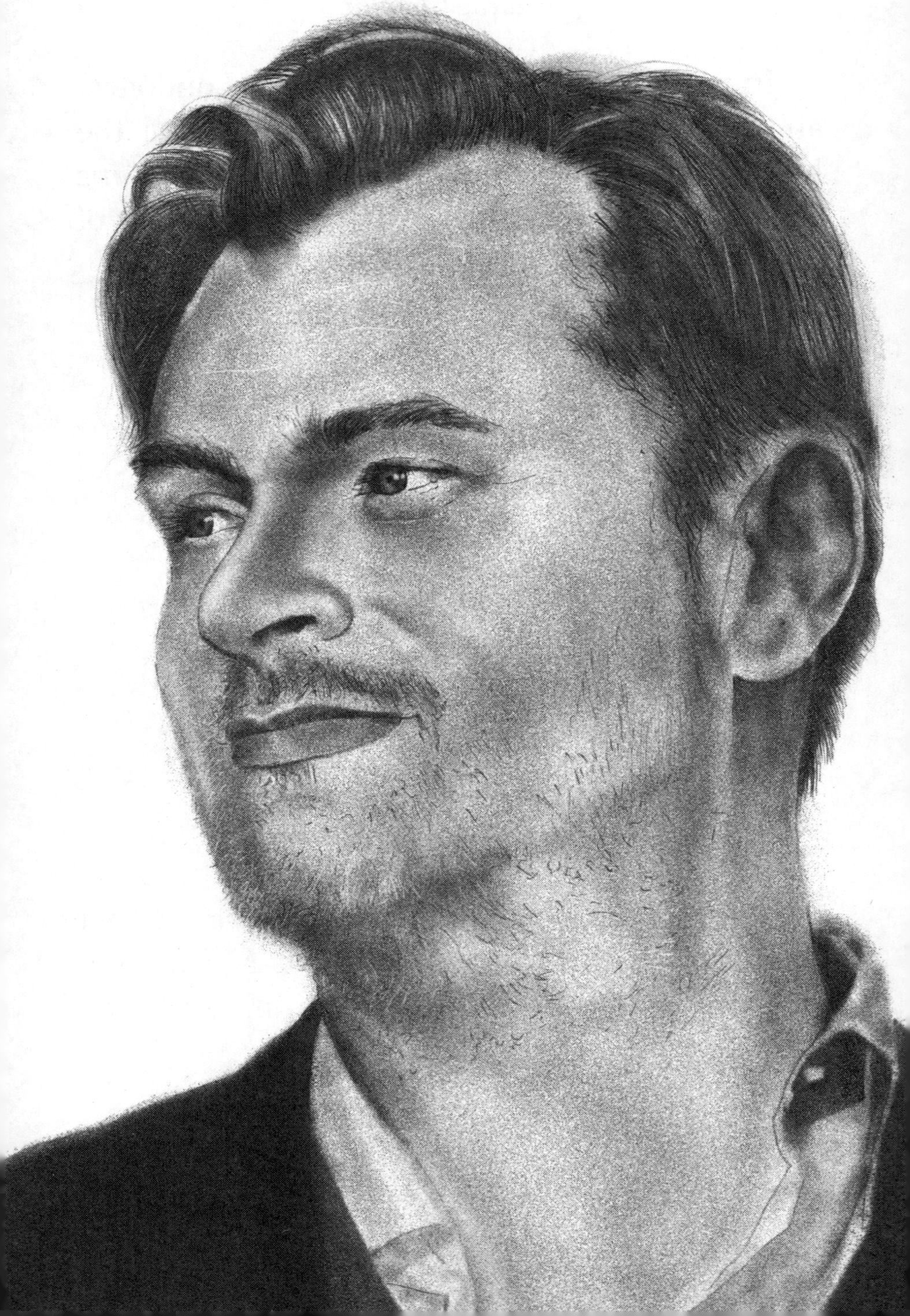

CHRISTOPHER NOLAN

BIRTH: July 30, 1970
Westminster, London, England

Christopher Nolan is one of the highest-grossing film directors and screenwriters in the world. He is both a British and an American citizen.

Christopher Edward Nolan was born in Westminster, London, on July 30, 1970. His father Brendan Nolan was an English ad man and his mother, Christina Nolan was an American flight attendant.

Nolan began shooting films at the age of seven.

George Lucas's *Star Wars* trilogy inspired him to pursue a film-making career. Nolan completed his education from University College London, where he studied English literature and was part of the film society. He created short films such as *Tarantella, Larceny* and *Doodlebug* during his college years.

Nolan's first full-length release was *Following*, in 1998. The plot revolved around a writer who kept getting involved in crimes with strange people in London. Nolan's masterpiece from 2000, *Memento*, a psychological thriller, was adapted from a short story written by his brother, Jonathan Nolan. It earned the Nolan brothers an Academy Award nomination for 'Best Original Screenplay'. His next project, also a psychological thriller, titled *Insomnia*, was about two detectives investigating a murder. It was a huge commercial success.

Warner Brothers enlisted Nolan's services for the *Batman* franchise in 2003. He directed *Batman Begins*, the first film from the *Dark Knight* trilogy, which released in 2005. It narrates the journey of Bruce Wayne as he becomes Batman and fights evil. The film received a nomination at the Academy Awards. Nolan's *The Dark Knight* (2008), the second movie of the trilogy, becoming on of the highest-grossing films.

In 2006, he released *The Prestige* starring Hugh Jackman, Christian Bale, Scarlett Johansson and others. It is a mysterious story of two musicians who become engaged in a lifelong battle full of deceit and darkness. Christopher Nolan's next release, which he also wrote, was *Inception*, starring Leonardo Di Caprio. It received four Academy Awards for its layered and thrilling tale about a corporate spy who thieves by intruding into people's subconsciousness. It is recognized as one of the best science-fiction films of all time.

The Dark Knight Rises released in 2012. It was the last movie of the *Dark Knight* trilogy. Nolan went on to co-write the Superman reboot *Man of Steel* with David S. Goyer.

In 2014, *Interstellar* was released, starring

Matthew McConaughey and Anne Hathaway. Nolan wrote, directed and produced this sci-fi drama about astronauts searching for another inhabitable place, besides Earth, where human survival is possible. The movie was nominated for four Academy Awards, and won one, in 2015.

Nolan and his brother Jonathan won the Waldo Salt Screenwriting Award for *Momento* in 2001. BAFTA awarded him the Britannica Award for Artistic Excellence in Directing in 2011, while The Visual Effects Society awarded him the VES Visionary Award.

He was the youngest director to be honored with a hand-and-footprint ceremony at Grauman's Chinese Theatre. In 2015, Nolan was honored with the Cinematic Imagery Award by The Art Directors Guild (ADG). His movies have been nominated a total of 26 times at the Academy Awards and won seven times.

Nolan's *Memento, The Dark Knight* and *Inception* were part of BBC's '100 Greatest Films of the 21st century'. His films were also featured in Empire magazine's 'The 100 Greatest Movies'. Nolan's *Dunkirk* was nominated at the Golden Globe awards in the 'Best Director' and 'Best Motion Picture Drama' categories.

Christopher Nolan has been married to Emma Thomas since 1997. They have three children. Emma Thomas is the co-producer of all of Nolan's films.

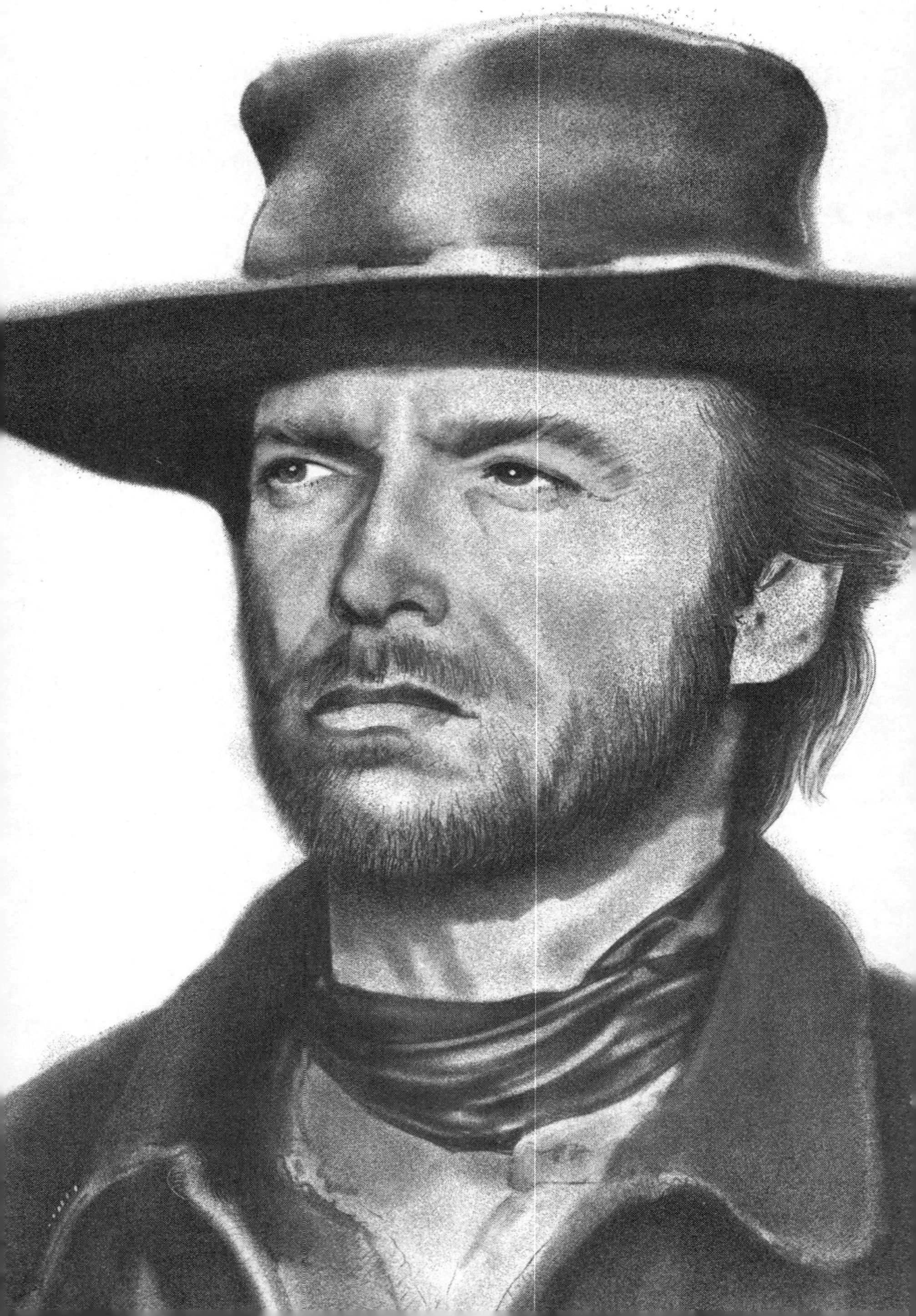

CLINT EASTWOOD

BIRTH: *May 31, 1930*
San Francisco, California, USA

Clint Eastwood is an American actor, director and producer. He has directed Academy Award-winning movies like *Unforgiven, Million Dollar Baby* and *Mystic River.*

Clinton Eastwood, Jr. was born on May 31, 1930, in San Francisco, California. His father Clinton, Sr. was a migrant worker, and his mother Ruth worked in a factory. Clinton was born during the Great Depression, and his parents had to take up odd jobs to support the family.

He completed his education from Piedmont Junior High School and Oakland Technical High School. He took up odd jobs in this period, such as being a lifeguard, a grocery clerk and a golf caddy to earn money for survival. After his graduation, Eastwood was drafted in the US Army during the Korean War and was stationed in California. He got discharged from duty in 1953.

Eastwood attended Los Angeles State University. But, he dropped out of college after just a year to pursue acting.

He got his first role with the Universal Studios after a screen-test in 1954. *Tarantula* and *Revenge of the Creature* were his first few movies, released in 1955. In 1959, Eastwood bagged a role as Rowdy Yates in the television series *Rawhide.*

Eastwood acquired international acclaim in 1964 by starring in the trio of Spaghetti Westerns directed by Sergio Leone—*A Fistful of Dollars, For A Few Dollars More,* and *The Good,*

The Bad and The Ugly.

Eastwood started directing with *Play Misty with Me* in 1971. Meanwhile, he continued acting in action series like *Dirty Harry*. He also ventured into comic roles with the 1974 film *Thunderbolt and Lightfoot,* and *Every Which Way but Loose* in 1978. His 1977 release, *The Gauntlet* was a formula action film in which he plays a cop. He also directed the film. The 1982 *Firefox,* a Cold War story, saw him acting as a pilot who stole from the Soviets. *Honkytonk Man* was also released in the same year. It is a story of a country singer with dreams, set during the Great Depression.

In 1988, he directed Charlie Parker's biopic called *Bird*. His 1992 film *Unforgiven* won the Academy Award for 'Best Picture' and 'Best Director'. Eastwood's *Mystic River* was released in 2003. He was given a Lifetime Achievement Award by the Screen Actors Guild in the same year.

Eastwood's 2004 direction of the unforgettable drama *Million Dollar Baby* won him two Academy Awards in the categories of 'Best Picture' and

'Best Direction'.

Eastwood collaborated with Steven Spielberg to produce *Flags of Our Fathers* and *Letters from Iwo Jima* in 2006. He directed the Broadway musical *Jersey Boys* in 2014. His movie *American Sniper* was released the same year. It was a biopic of the Navy SEAL Operator, Chris Kyle. Eastwood once again directed a biopic, *Sully*, which was released in 2016. Tom Hanks and Eastwood were both commended for this film.

Eastwood has been justifiably honored with many awards and nominations. He has received Directors Guild of America Awards, Golden Globes, Academy Awards and People's Choice Awards. In 2009, he was given the Lumiere Award and was honored with Légion d'honneur, France's highest civilian distinction. Eastwood has been inducted to the California Hall of Fame. In 2013, he won the Golden Pine Lifetime Achievement Award.

Clint Eastwood has been married twice. His

first marriage was to Maggie Johnson, from 1953 to 1982. His second marriage was to American television anchor Dina Ruiz, in 1996. They separated in 2013.

Clint Eastwood is an animal rights activist. He also supports charities such as City of Hope, American Heart Association, Artists for Peace and Justice, and Unite for Japan. Eastwood has also served as a mayor of Carmel-by-the-Sea in California.

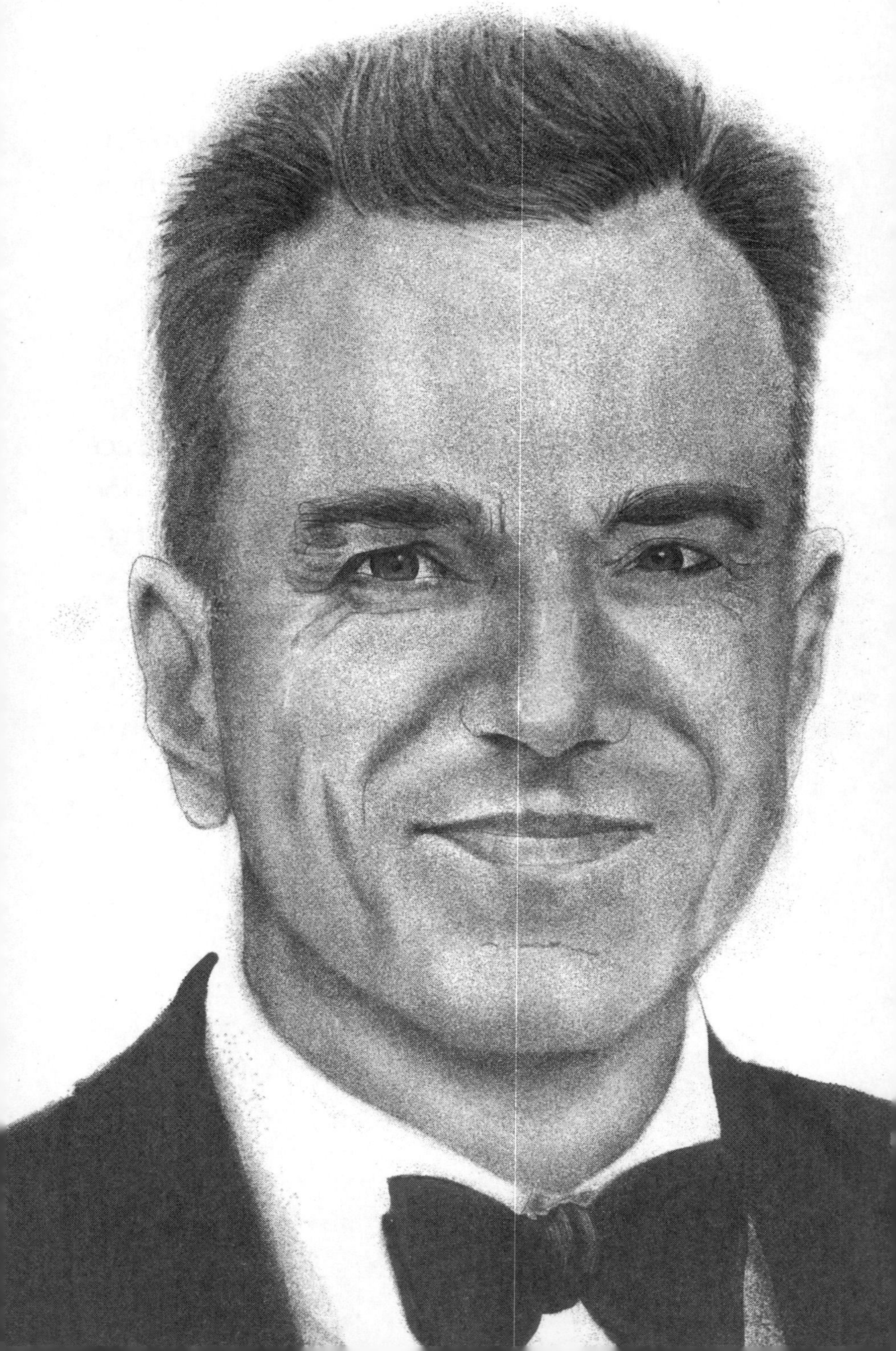

DANIEL DAY-LEWIS

BIRTH: April 29, 1957
Kensington, London, England

Sir Daniel Day-Lewis was born on April 29, 1957 in London, England. His father, Cecil Day-Lewis, was a poet laureate of the United Kingdom. His mother, Jill Balcon, was an actor. His older sister, Tamasin, is a television writer and documentary filmmaker.

Day-Lewis studied at Sevenoaks School and Bedales. He began to learn acting at the Bristol Old Vic Theatre School. He made his film debut at the age of fourteen in *Sunday Bloody Sunday* in 1971.

He joined the Royal Shakespeare Company. Lewis played Romeo in *Romeo and Juliet* and Flute in *A Midsummer Night's Dream*. In 1982, he bagged a minor role in *Gandhi* and finally returned to the screen. He was a part of the casts of *Frost in May* and *How Many Miles to Babylon*. In 1984, he worked alongside Anthony Hopkins and Sir Laurence Oliver in The Bounty. He appeared in *A Room with a View* in 1986. His performance in the movie gained him much critical acclaim.

In 1987, he bagged the lead role in *The Unbearable Lightness of Being*. He learned Czech in order to play a Czech surgeon in the movie. He played the character of Christy Brown in *My Left Foot* in 1989. His performance in this film earned him his first Academy Award, alongside a BAFTA Award for 'Best Actor'. Throughout the course of filming, he sat in a wheel chair and even learnt to paint with his left foot.

In 1989, Day-Lewis worked at the National Theatre in London with Richard Eyre for Hamlet. This was followed by movies such as

The Last of the Mohicans and *The Age of Innocence*. *The Age of Innocence*, which released in 1993, is an adaptation of Edith Wharton's Novel by the novel of the same name. *In the Name of the Father* released in 1993, and is the story of a young Irish boy wrongly accused of the 1974 IRA bombings in UK. The movie won him an Academy Award nomination. *The Crucible*, which released in 1996, is based on Arthur Miller's play by the same name.

Day-Lewis took a break after this and moved to Italy to work as a cobbler's apprentice. He returned to the big screen after five years with Martin Scorsese's *Gangs of New York*. He played the character of Bill the Butcher alongside Leonardo DiCaprio in this epic period drama set in the slums of New York. In 2007, he acted in *There Will Be Blood*. In 2009, he starred in Rob Marshall's romantic musical drama *Nine*.

In 2012, Day-Lewis portrayed the sixteenth president of United States, Abraham Lincoln in Steven Spielberg's *Lincoln*. It was based on a book by Doris Kearns Goodwin. He won an Academy Award for 'Best Actor'.

In 2017, he worked on his final film, *Phantom Thread*, directed by Paul Thomas Anderson. It was a period drama depicting the world of fashion in London. The same year, a spokesperson of Day-Lewis announced his retirement from acting.

Day-Lewis has been a recipient of many awards and accolades for his works. He has been honored with three Academy Awards for his performances in *My Left Foot, Lincoln* and *There Will Be Blood*. He has received four British Academy of Film and Television Arts Awards for 'Best Actor'. He is also a recipient of two Golden Globe Awards and three Screen Star Actors Guild Awards.

In 2012, he was honored by *Time* magazine as the 'World's Greatest Actor'. He was knighted by Prince William at the Buckingham Palace in 2014 .

Day-Lewis married the filmmaker and novelist Rebecca Miller in 1996. They have two sons together. He had another son with French actor

Isabelle Adjani.

Day-Lewis is known for his selective movie performances. He has starred in just six movies since 1998. He is renowned for his method acting and dedication to the characters. Day-Lewis was even included in People magazine's '50 Most Beautiful People in the World' in 2013.

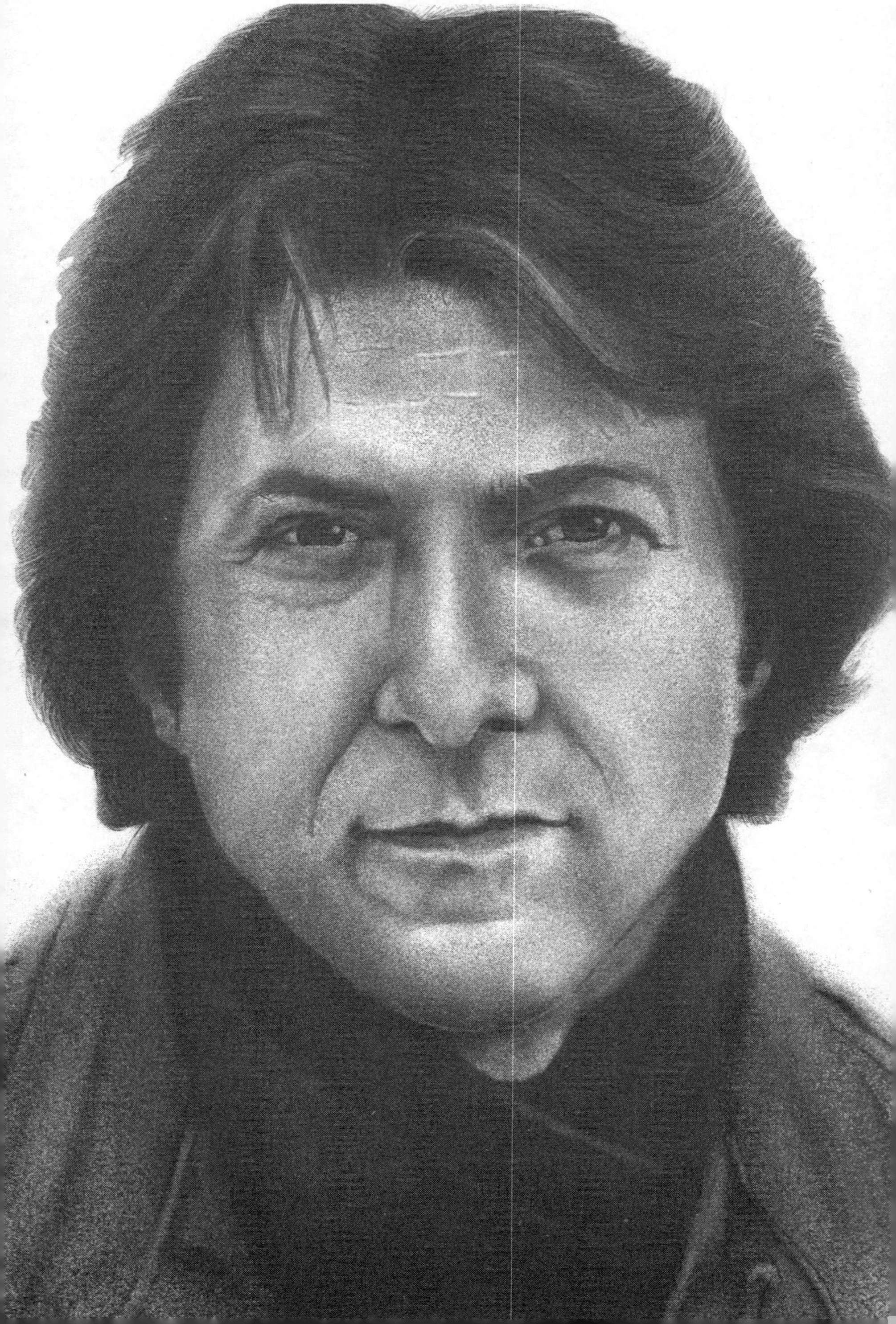

DUSTIN HOFFMAN

BIRTH: *August 8, 1937*
Los Angeles, California, USA

Dustin Hoffman is an American actor and director. This Oscar-winning actor is best known for his roles in *The Graduate, Rain Man* and *Kramer vs. Kramer.*

Dustin Lee Hoffman was born on August 8, 1937, in Los Angeles, California, to Lillian and Harry Hoffman. His father was a furniture salesman and prop supervisor at Columbia Pictures.

Hoffman had joined Santa Monica College to study music. But he quit college at the age of 19 to pursue a career in acting. He joined the Pasadena Playhouse and became friends with Gene Hackman. Both of them left for New York together to search for work in the television industry.

Through the 1960s, Hoffman acted in some off-Broadway productions and studied method acting at the Actors Studio. In 1965, he performed in Henry Livings' *Eh?* His first theatrical film was *The Tiger Makes Out*, in 1967.

In 1967, he landed a role in *The Graduate*, portraying the character Benjamin Braddock in the romantic comedy-drama. It received Academy Award nominations and Golden Globe nominations. In the following year, Hoffman acted in the Broadway production *Jimmy Shine*, and received a Drama Desk Award for this role. Hoffman played the role of Ratso Rizzo in the 1969 movie *Midnight Cowboy*. He won an Academy Award for his performance.

Hoffman's memorable movies from the 1970s include *Straw Dogs* and *Papillon*. He earned another Academy Award nomination for his role in *Lenny* in 1974. In 1979, *Kramer vs. Kramer* was released. Hoffman won an Academy Award for his role as a workaholic father.

Hoffman did a television movie, an adaptation of Arthur Miller's *Death of a Salesman* in 1985. He received an Emmy and a Golden Globe for this. In 1988, Hoffman acted as an autistic savant in *Rain Man*. He received his second Academy Award for this performance. Hoffman acted alongside Sean Connery and Mathew Broderick in *Family Business* in 1989.

In 1997, he acted alongside Robert De Niro in the political satire *Wag the Dog*. It is a black comedy film about an American President orchestrating a war to avoid media attention over a scandal. This movie got him his seventh Academy Award nomination.

In 2003, Hoffman worked with a friend from his initial years of struggle, Gene Hackman, in

Runaway Jury. He worked with Robert De Niro once again in *Meet the Fockers* in 2004. He was also a part of its sequel, *Little Fockers* in 2010.

Hoffman lent his voice to the beloved character Shifu in the *Kung Fu Panda* franchise. It won him the Annie Award for 'Voice Acting in an Animated Feature'. In 2008, he voiced the character of Roscuro in the animated fantasy film, *The Tale of Despereaux*. In 2012, he made his debut as a director with the comedy-drama *Quartet*.

Hoffman has been nominated for seven Academy Awards so far. Out of these, he won two for *Kramer vs. Kramer* and *Rain Man*. He has received three BAFTA awards, five Golden Globes and one New York Film Critic Award. He has been honored with David di Donatello awards four times. Hoffman was awarded the Cecil B. DeMille Award by the Golden Globes. For his contribution to cinema, he was honored with the American Film Institute's Life Achievement Award in 1999. In 2012, Hoffman was honored with the Kennedy Center Honors

Award.

Hoffman has been married twice. His first marriage was to actor Anne Byrne. They separated in 1980. He then married businesswoman Lisa Gottsegen. He is the father of six children. His son, Jake Hoffman, is also an actor and a writer.

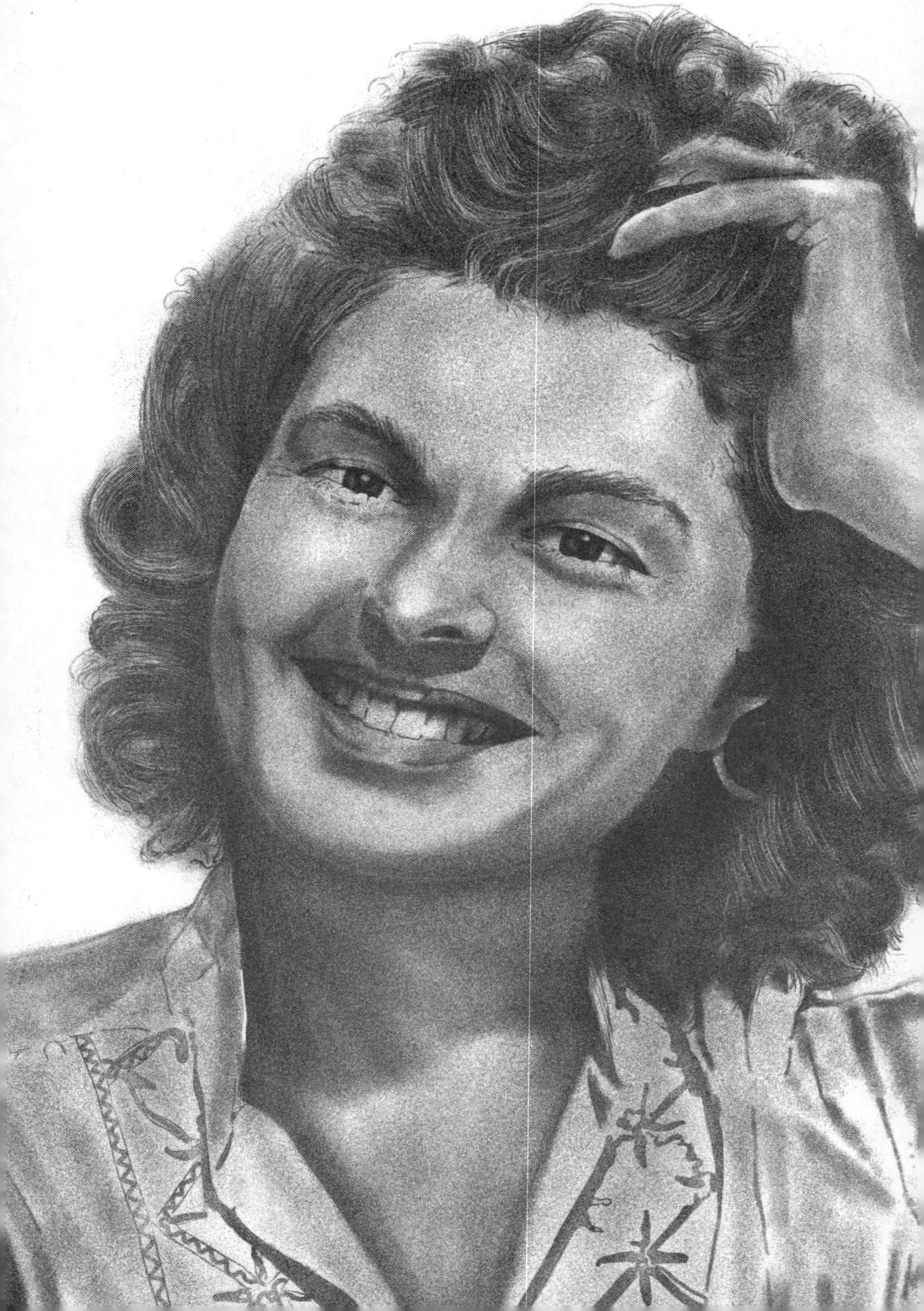

INGRID BERGMAN

BIRTH: *August 29, 1915*
Stockholm, Sweden

DEATH: *August 29, 1982 (aged 67)*
London, England

Ingrid Bergman was a Swedish actress and a star in American and European cinema. She is still remembered for her brilliant performances in *Casablanca* and *Spellbound*.

Ingrid Bergman was born in Stockholm, Sweden, on August 29, 1915. She was born to a Swedish father, Justus Bergman, and a German mother, Friedel. Both her parents passed away when she was a young child. She was raised by her uncle and aunt. She studied in a private school and regularly performed in school plays. She received a state scholarship to the Royal Dramatic Theatre School in the 1930s. She left the theater a year later when she got hired by a Swedish film studio.

Bergman made her debut in films in 1935 with *Munkbrogreven (The Count from the Monk's Bridge)*. In 1936, she acted in the romantic drama *Intermezzo*. She also starred in the English version of this movie, *Intermezzo: A Love Story*, made by the American film producer David O. Selznick, in 1939. It gained her recognition amongst the Hollywood audience and peers.

In 1940, she acted in *Juninatten (A Night in June)*. She then played the role of a governess in *Adam Had Four Sons* in 1941. It was the role of Ilsa Lund in *Casablanca* in 1942 that earned her widespread popularity and praise. She starred opposite Humphrey Bogart and Paul Henreid in this romantic drama. The movie received consistently good reviews and is still considered to be relevant, and has only grown in popularity in the past decades.

In 1943, Bergman appeared as Maria in the film adaptation of Ernest Hemingway's *For Whom the Bell Tolls*. This was her first film in color. Bergman then starred in George D. Cukor's *Gaslight* in 1944. Her performance in this movie earned her her first Academy Award.

She worked with Alfred Hitchcock in thrillers such as *Spellbound* and *Notorious*. Her role as the spy Alicia Huberman in *Notorious* received much critical acclaim. She also worked in the 1946 Broadway production of *Joan of Lorraine* for which she received a Tony award.

Bergman returned to American cinema with *Anastasia* in 1956. Her role in this movie earned her another Academy Award. In 1958, she starred opposite Cary Grant in the romantic comedy, *Indiscreet*.

In 1974, Bergman bagged another Academy Award for her role in the British-American film adaptation of Agatha Christie's *Murder on the*

Orient Express. She starred in the musical drama *Autumn Sonata* directed by Ingmar Bergman in 1978. Her last performance was in 1981, in the television movie *A Woman Called Golda.* She portrayed the Israeli leader Golda Meir for this movie.

Bergman is a recipient of three Academy Awards, four Golden Globe Awards, two Primetime Emmy Awards, a Tony and a BAFTA. She was awarded at the National Board of Review Awards four times. The National Society of Film Critics honored her with the 'Best Actress' award for her role in *Autumn Sonata.* She has been awarded by the New York Film Critics Circle thrice.

In 1952, Bergman was honored with the Volpi Cup for 'Best Actress' by the Venice Film Festival. She received the Honorary Cesar at the Cesar Awards in 1976. She was ranked the fourth-greatest female screen legend by the American Film Institute in 1999.

Bergman was inducted to the Hollywood Walk of Fame in 1960. In 1980, her autobiography titled *Ingrid Bergman: My Story* was published. David Seymour's photograph of Ingrid Bergman was selected as the poster for the 2015 Cannes Film Festival, as it was her birth anniversary year.

The documentary *Ingrid Bergman: In Her Own Words,* too was screened at this festival. Ingrid Bergman got married three times. She first married Dr. Peter Lindstrom in 1937. Then she got married to the Italian director Roberto Rossellini in 1950. They divorced in 1957. Bergman married theatrical entrepreneur Lars Schmidt in 1958. They too separated in 1975. She was a mother of four children. She passed away at the age of 67 on August 29, 1982, due to breast cancer.

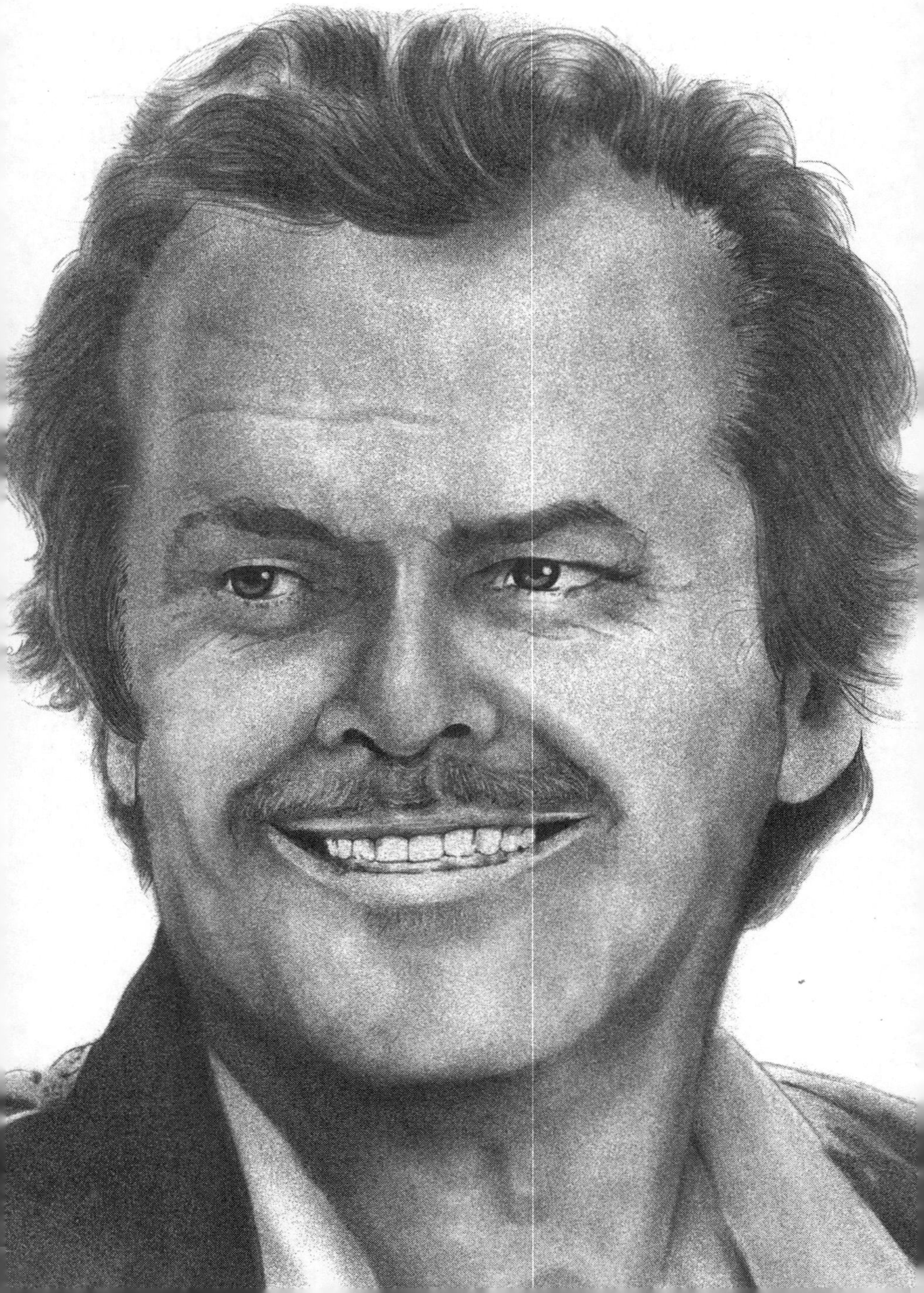

JACK NICHOLSON

BIRTH: *April 22, 1937*
New Jersey, USA

Jack Nicholson is an American actor and filmmaker. His most celebrated films include *Easy Rider, One Flew Over the Cuckoo's Nest, The Shining* and *The Bucket List*. Apart from being known as an actor, he is also the director of three phenomenal films, including the sequel to Chinatown called *The Two Jakes*, released in 1990.

Jack Nicholson was born on April 22, 1937, in Neptune, New Jersey. His mother, June

Nicholson, worked as a showgirl. His maternal grandparents, John and Ethel May, raised him.

Nicholson moved to Los Angeles and worked at a toy store and at the animation department of the MGM Studios. He performed with the Playing Ring Theatre in 1957.

Nicholson bagged a leading role in *The Cry Baby Killer* in 1958. In the 1960s, he appeared in low-budget movies such as *The Terror, Ride in the Whirlwind,* and *The Shooting.* In 1967, he wrote the screenplay for *The Trip.* In 1969, he played the role of the lawyer George Hanson in *Easy Rider.* This role earned him an Academy Award nomination for 'Best Supporting Actor'. He acted as a musical prodigy in *Five Easy Pieces* in 1970. This earned him another Academy Award nomination, this time in the category of 'Best Actor'.

Nicholson played a detective in Roman Polanski's *Chinatown* in 1974. This was followed by *One Flew Over the Cuckoo's Nest.* The movie was based on Ken Kesey's novel of the same name.

Nicholson finally received his first Academy Award for this role. In 1980, Nicholson delivered the most remarkable performance of his career, as a hotel caretaker in the movie adaptation of Stephen King's novel *The Shining*, by Stanley Kubrick.

Other movies of his from the 1980s include *Reds, Ironweed* and *Terms of Endearment*. In 1989, Nicholson was cast in *Batman* and played the iconic character of the Joker. This film was a commercial hit. In 1992, he delivered another gratifying performance in *A Few Good Men*. In 1997, he was awarded his third Academy Award for *As Good as it Gets*.

In the early 2000s, he acted in movies such as *About Schmidt, Anger Management* and *Something's Gotta Give*. In 2006, Nicholson appeared alongside Matt Damon and Leonardo DiCaprio in *The Departed*, a crime thriller directed by Martin Scorsese. He starred opposite Morgan Freeman in the feel-good comedy drama *The Bucket List* in 2007.

Nicholson is the most-nominated male actor in the Academy's history with twelve nominations. But won the honors only thrice. He won the Acaemy Award for 'Best Actor' for *One Flew Over the Cuckoo's Nest* and *As Good as it Gets*. He also won the Academy Award for 'Best Supporting Actor' for *Terms of Endearment*. He is one of the few actors who has been nominated for an Oscar in every decade of his career (from the 1960s to the 2000s).

Nicholson has been awarded seven Golden Globe Awards. In 2001, the Kennedy Center Honor was bestowed upon him. He was also awarded the Lifetime Achievement Award by the American Film Institute. In 2008, he got inducted to the California Hall of Fame. He was inducted into the New Jersey Hall of Fame in 2010. Nicholson took part in the 2001 telethon called 'America: A Tribute to Heroes' to raise funds in support of the victims of 9/11.

Nicholson married actress Sandra Knight in 1962. They had a daughter called Jennifer, and the couple went on to get divorced in 1968. Nicholson has fathered five children. His daughter, Lorraine Nicholson, is also an actor.

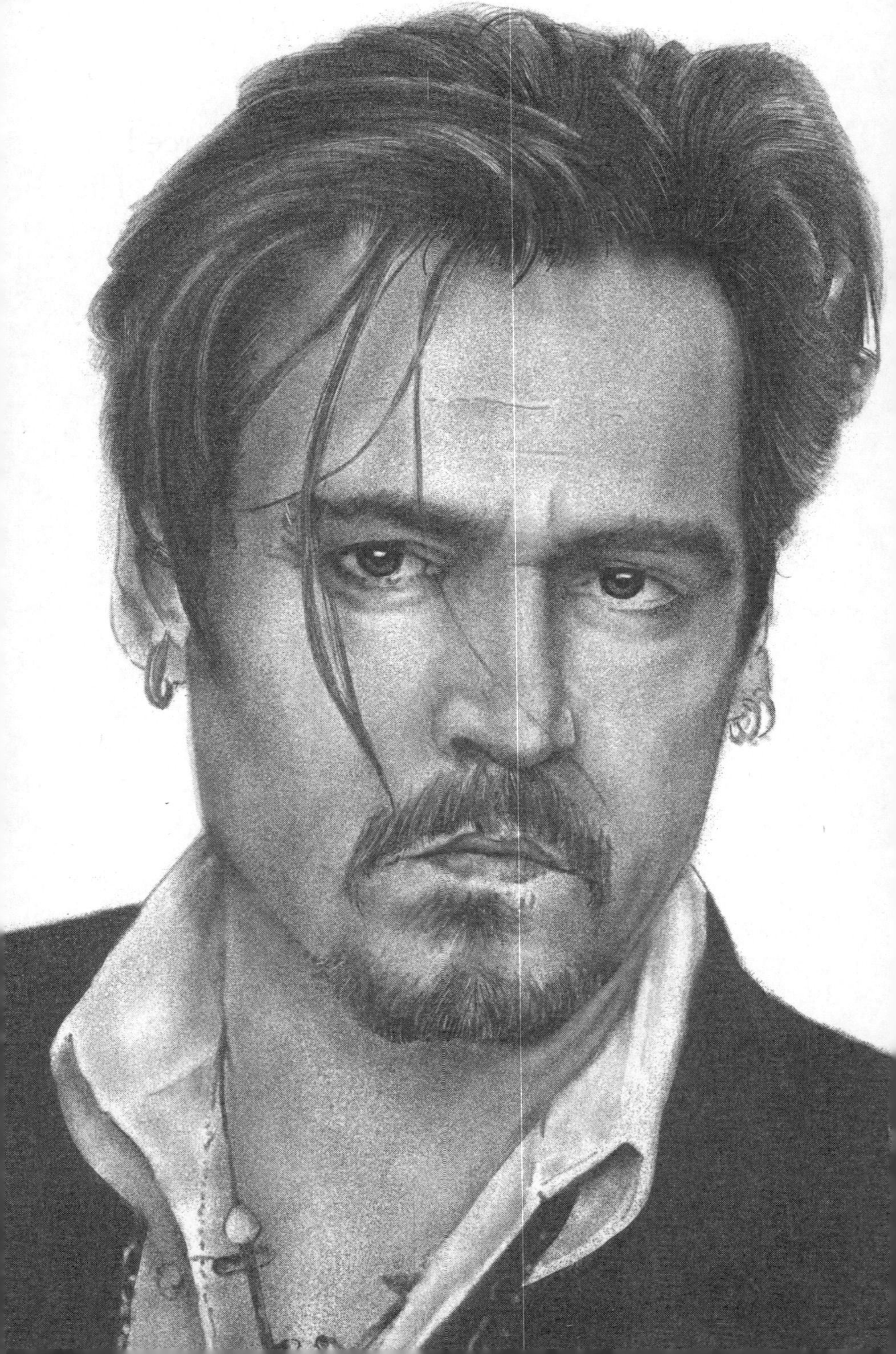

JOHNNY DEPP

BIRTH: June 9, 1963
Kentucky, USA

Johnny Depp is an American actor, producer and musician. He is known for his characteristic eccentric roles in movies like *Ed Wood* and *Charlie and the Chocolate Factory*. However, he's globally known for playing the character Jack Sparrow in the *Pirates of the Caribbean* series.

Johnny Depp was born as John Christopher Depp II on June 9, 1963, in Owensboro, Kentucky, to John and Betty Sue Depp. His father, John, was a civil engineer. His mother, Betty Sue, worked as a waitress. He was the youngest of four siblings. His mother gifted him a guitar when he was twelve years old, thus nurturing a love for music in the young Depp. His parents divorced when he was fifteen years old.

Depp dropped out of high school to pursue a career in music. He moved to Los Angeles and joined a band. They got a record deal with Geffen Records in 1986. In the 1980s, Nicolas Cage then encouraged Depp to pursue acting and introduced him to an agent.

Depp landed his first role in the 1984 horror movie *The Nightmare on Elm Street*. His next role was in Oliver Stone's Platoon. He made his television debut in 1987, playing an undercover cop, Tom Hanson, in the hit television series *21 Jump Street*. In 1990, he acted in the movie *Cry Baby*. It wasn't a commercial success at the time but has gained cult status over time.

In 1990, he acted in Tim Burton's fantasy movie, *Edward Scissorhands*. Depp started getting recognition as an A-list actor after this project. In 1994, Depp once again acted in Tim Burton's *Ed Wood*. It was a biopic of the American director Ed Wood. Depp got nominated at the Golden Globes for his performance. Depp starred in *Don Juan DeMarco* in 1994, portraying a character who believed himself to be Don Juan.

In 2003, Depp was cast in his most iconic role, Captain Jack Sparrow in the *Pirates of the Caribbean* franchise. He was nominated for an Academy Award for his portrayal of a pirate. He starred in the *Secret Window* in 2004, based on Stephen King's novella *Secret Window, Secret Garden*.

Depp played the eccentric Willy Wonka in the adaptation of Roald Dahl's *Charlie and the Chocolate Factory* in 2005. He also gave voice to Victor van Dort in Tim Burton's *Corpse Bride*. In 2006 and 2007, the actor went on to play Captain Jack Sparrow once again in *Pirates of the Caribbean: Dead Man's Chest* and *Pirates of the Caribbean: At World's End*.

In 2007, he again collaborated with Tim

Burton in *Sweeney Todd: The Demon Barber of Fleet Street*. He followed this up with another remarkable character, playing the Mad Hatter in Burton's *Alice in Wonderland*. In 2011, Captain Jack Sparrow returned in *Pirates of the Caribbean: On Stranger Tides*.

In Burton's version of *Dark Shadows*, Depp played Barnabas Collins. He acted opposite Armie Hammer in *The Lone Ranger* in 2013. Depp revisited another one of his roles in 2016, as the Mad Hatter, in Tim Burton's *Through the Looking Glass*.

One of his first awards—of the many Depp has received—was the 'Actor of the Year' award from the London Film Critics' Circle in 1996. He was awarded France's National Film Award, the Caesar, in 1999. He received a star at the Hollywood Walk of Fame in the same year. He won a Golden Globe for 'Best Actor' for *Sweeney Todd* and was declared 'Best Villain' by the MTV Movie Awards in 2008.

Depp won the People's Choice Award for

'Favorite Movie Actor' consistently from 2010 to 2014. In 2012, he was recorded as the highest-paid actor by Guinness World Records. He was nominated for Academy Awards thrice. He has won the Screen Actors Guild Award for 'Outstanding Actor in a Leading Role'.

Depp has been married twice. His last marriage was with actress Amber Heard in 2015. They got divorced the following year. Depp also has two children with the French singer Vanessa Paradis.

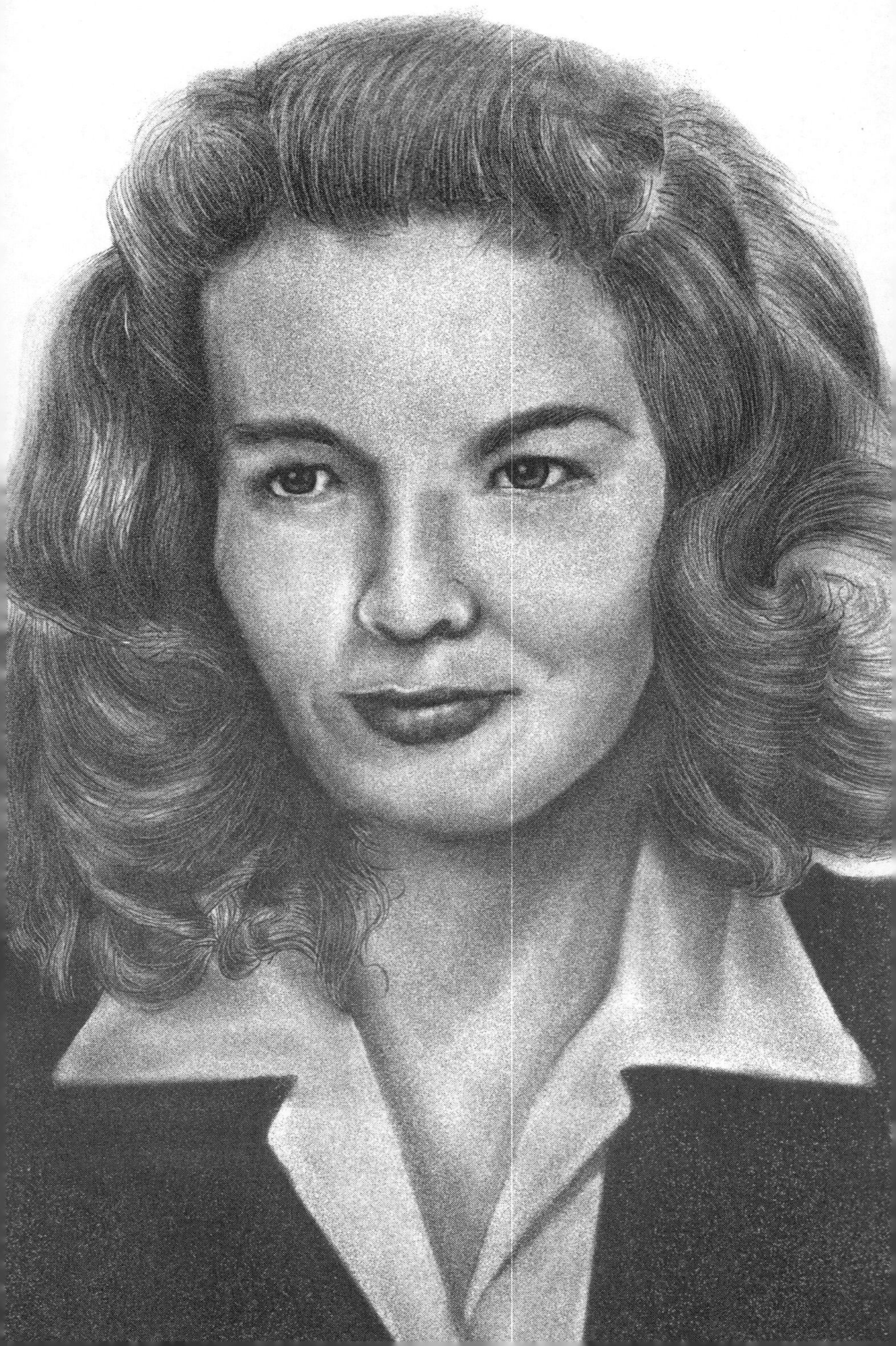

KATHARINE HEPBURN

BIRTH: *May 12, 1907*
Hartford, Connecticut, USA

DEATH: *June 29, 2003 (aged 96)*
Fenwick, Connecticut, USA

Katharine Houghton Hepburn was an American actress named as the greatest female star of classic Hollywood cinema by the American Film Institute. She is known for her memorable performances in *The African Queen, On Golden Pond,* and *Guess Who's Coming to Dinner.*

Katharine Hepburn was born on May 12, 1907 in Hartford, Connecticut, to Thomas Hepburn and Katharine Martha. She attended the Bryn Mawr College in 1924 and graduated in 1928.

She made her Broadway debut in '*Night Hostess*'. She was cast in the lead role in Broadway's *The Warrior's Husband* in 1932.

In 1932, Hepburn debuted opposite John Barrymore in *A Bill of Divorcement*. The following year, she acted in *Christopher Strong*. She played the role of Eva Lovelace in *Morning Glory* in 1933. In the same year, she appeared as Jo in the film adaptation of Louisa May Alcott's classic novel *Little Women*. In the 1930s, she acted in various films such as *The Little Minister, Sylvia Scarlett, Alice Adams* and *Quality Street*.

In 1938, Hepburn played Tracy Lord in Philip Barry's stage play *The Philadelphia Story*. The following year, she reprised the role of Tracy Lord for a film production based on the play. This earned her a nomination at the Academy Awards. Spencer Tracy and Hepburn co-starred in Women of the Year in 1942. This was their first film together. The duo continued to share the screen in the following years, in *Keeper of the Flame, Without Love* and *Adam's Rib.*

Hepburn took up more challenging roles in the 1950s with *The African Queen* and *Pat and Mike.* She received Academy Award nominations for her roles in *The African Queen, Summertime, The Rainmaker* and Suddenly, *Last Summer.*

Hepburn and Tracy also worked together in *Guess Who's Coming to Dinner* in 1967. Hepburn won an Academy Award for 'Best Actress' for this performance. She earned another Academy Award for *The Lion in Winter* in 1968.

Hepburn acted in many Broadway product-ions during the 1970s and 1980s. She portrayed Coco Chanel, the legendary French designer, in the Broadway musical *Coco.* One of her significant movies from this time was *On Golden Pond.* In 1994, she made her last appearance in *One Christmas.*

Hepburn took up more challenging roles in the 1950s with *The African Queen* and *Pat and Mike.* She received Academy Award nominations for her roles in *The African Queen, Summertime,*

The Rainmaker and *Suddenly, Last Summer.*

Hepburn and Tracy also worked together in *Guess Who's Coming to Dinner* in 1967. Hepburn won an Academy Award for 'Best Actress' for this performance. She earned another Academy Award for *The Lion in Winter* in 1968.

Hepburn acted in many Broadway productions during the 1970s and 1980s. She portrayed Coco Chanel, the legendary French designer, in the Broadway musical *Coco*. One of her significant movies from this time was *On Golden Pond*. In 1994, she made her last appearance in *One Christmas*.

Katharine Hepburn holds the record of the most Academy Awards won in the 'Best Actress' category. She was the recipient of four Academy Awards and was nominated eight more times. She won two British Academy Film Awards and was even honored with awards at the Cannes Film Festival and the Venice Film Festival. She has also been awarded by the New York Critics Circle and the People's Choice Awards.

Hepburn was awarded an Emmy in 1975 for her performance in the television film called *Love Among the Ruins*. In 1980, she received the Lifetime Achievement Award from the Screen Actors Guild. In the same year, she was inducted to the American Theater Hall of Fame. Hepburn was bestowed with the Kennedy Center Honors in 1990. The American Film Institute declared her the greatest film star of classic Hollywood cinema in 1999.

Hepburn has been included in Ros Horton and Sally Simmons' book *Women Who Changed the World*. Encyclopedia Britannica also includes her in their list of '300 Women Who Changed the World'. Many of her films are part of the '100 Greatest Films of all time' list by the American Film Institute.

Hepburn married businessman Ludlow Ogden Smith in 1928. They divorced in 1934. She never married again but she was in a long-term relationship with her co-star Spencer Tracy. Hepburn passed away on June 29, 2003, at the age of 96.

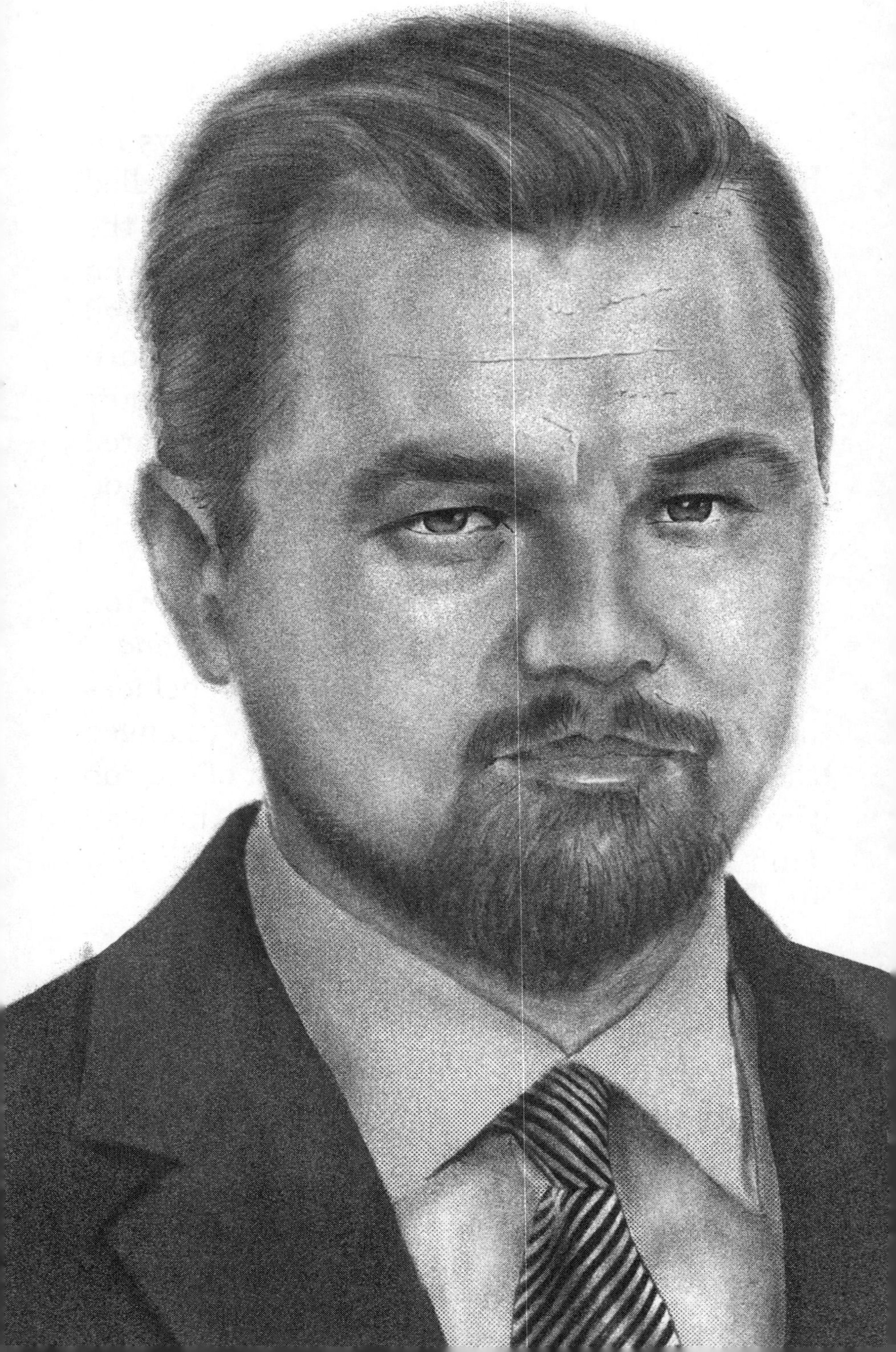

LEONARDO DICAPRIO

BIRTH: *November 11, 1974*
California, USA

Leonardo DiCaprio is one of the most respected American actors and producers in Hollywood. He is best known for his timeless roles in *Titanic, The Wolf of Wall Street* and *The Revenant*.

Leonardo Wilhelm DiCaprio was born on November 11, 1974 in California, to Irmelin and George DiCaprio. His parents got divorced when he was merely a year old. His mother raised him.

DiCaprio did his preliminary schooling from

Seeds Elementary School. He attended John Marshall High School for three years and left with a general equivalent diploma.

When he was five years old, DiCaprio began acting in the children's television series *Romper Room*. He worked in television shows such as *The New Lassie* and *Roseanne* as a teenager. He was a part of the 1990 comedy series called *Parenthood*.

His first movie, called *Critters 3*, released in 1991. In 1993, he acted opposite Robert De Niro in *The Boy's Life*, an adaptation of Tobias Wolff's memoir. It was received well by the critics. *What's Eating Gilbert Grape* released the same year. DiCaprio starred alongside Johnny Depp in this movie. It earned him an Academy Award nomination.

In 1996, DiCaprio played Romeo in Baz Luhrmann's Romeo + Juliet, inspired by Shakespeare's original play. DiCaprio's career reached new heights in 1997 when he and Kate Winslet starred in the tragic love story *Titanic*, created by James Cameron. It was the movie with the highest budget at the time. His character, Jack Dawson remains his most remembered role. The movie won eleven Academy Awards.

In 2002, he acted in Steven Spielberg's *Catch Me if You Can* and Martin Scorsese's *Gangs of New York*. DiCaprio founded a production company called Appian Way Production in 2004. In 2006, he was a part of *Blood Diamond* and *The Departed*. Being a champion of environmental causes, he wrote an environmental documentary in 2007, called *The 11th Hour*.

DiCaprio acted in Christopher Nolan's brilliant thriller *Inception* in 2010. He also starred in Scorsese's *Shutter Island* in the same year. He played Jay Gatsby in Luhrmann's adaptation of Fitzgerald's *The Great Gatsby*. DiCaprio collaborated with Scorsese again in the 2013 movie *The Wolf of Wall Street*.

In 2015, DiCaprio starred in Alejandro González Iñárritu's *The Revenant*. It was based on a novel by Michael Punke. DiCaprio played the frontiersman, Hugh Glass. He earned many prestigious awards for his chilling performance, including an Academy Award.

DiCaprio has received more than fifty awards for his work. He won Golden Globes for his performances in *The Aviator* and *The Revenant*. He won an Academy Award and a BAFTA award for *The Revenant*. His performance in *The Wolf of Wall Street* earned him a Golden Globe in the category of 'Best Actor—Motion Picture Musical or Comedy'.

DiCaprio is a strong supporter of many environmental organizations. He is on the board of the World Wildlife Fund, Natural Resources Defense Council and International Fund for Animal Welfare. He is also associated with Global Green USA. In 2000, he hosted Earth Day festivities and interviewed US president Bill Clinton on issues related to global warming. He expressed his environmental concerns and views at the American segment of Live Earth in 2007. In 2014, he was appointed as the United Nations representative for climate change. DiCaprio regularly donates to the Wildlife Conservation Society.

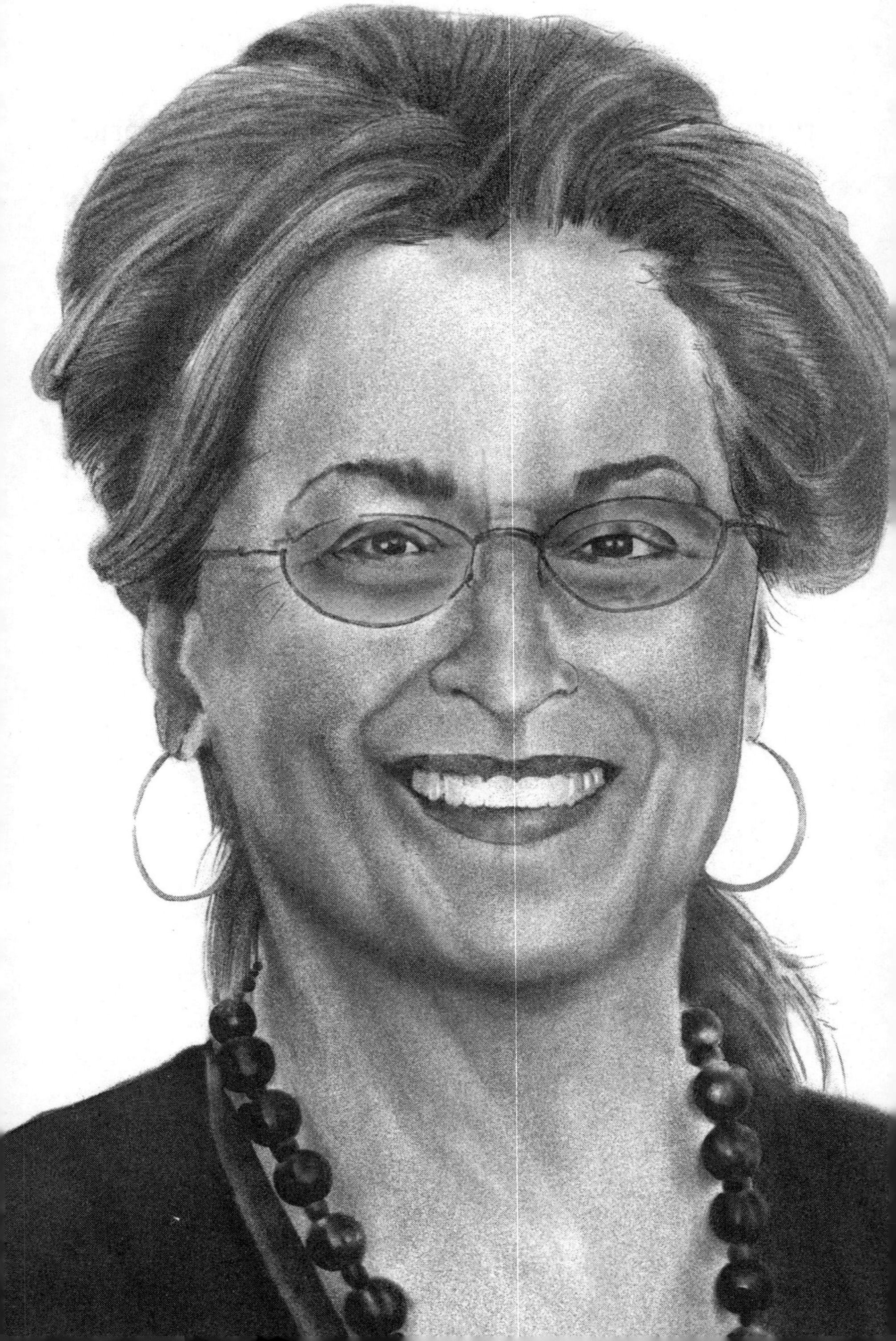

MERYL STREEP

BIRTH: June 22, 1949
Summit, New Jersey, USA

Mary Louise "Meryl" Streep is an American actress, considered to be one of the best actresses of her generation. She is known for her roles in iconic films such as *The Devil Wears Prada, Mamma Mia!, The Deer Hunter* and *Doubt.*

Meryl Streep was born on June 22, 1949 in Summit, New Jersey. Her mother, Mary Wolf, was a commercial artist. Her father, Harry William Streep, was a pharmaceutical executive.

Streep did her Bachelors in Drama from

Vassar College. She also received an MFA Degree from Yale School of Drama. During this time, she made her debut on stage.

Streep performed for various theater companies in New York and New Jersey. She also performed at the New York Shakespeare Festival. She was a part of the Broadway production of *Happy End*. In 1976, she appeared in a double bill of Tennessee Williams' *27 Wagons Full of Cotton*. In 1977, she participated in the revival of Anton Chekhov's *The Cherry Orchard*.

Streep landed her first role in a feature film with *Julia* in 1977. She also appeared in the television series *Holocaust*. She earned her first Academy nomination in 1978 with the release of *Deer Hunter*.

The family drama *Kramer vs. Kramer* earned Streep her first Academy Award, for 'Best Supporting Actress'. She also received an Oscar for *Sophie's Choice* in 1983. In the same year, Streep acted in the psychological thriller, *Still of the Night*.

Streep was part of the movie adaptation of Carrie Fisher's novel *Postcards from the Edge* in 1990. She acted opposite Clint Eastwood in the romantic drama *The Bridges of Madison County*. She received another Oscar for Wes Craven's *Music of the Heart*, in which she played the character of a music teacher who taught in New York's Harlem neighborhood. It was based on a true story.

Streep acted in Steven Spielberg's *Artificial Intelligence: AI* in 2001. The movie garnered much commercial success. She returned to the stage in the same year with Mike Nicholas' reproduction of Chekhov's *The Seagull*. In 2003, she earned her second Emmy for the television adaptation of the play *Angels in America*.

She starred in the fantasy adventure *A Series of Unfortunate Events*, and the political thriller *The Manchurian Candidate*, both in 2004.

Streep's most commercially acclaimed movie, *The Devil Wears Prada*, was released in 2006. Her performance as the most prolific fashion magazine editor in the city, Miranda Priestly, earned her

Golden Globe and Academy Award nominations. She played the character of Yolanda Johnson in Altman's *A Prairie Home Companion*. She portrayed Donna in the musical *Mamma Mia!* and reprised this role in the sequel in 2018.

Streep received an Academy Award and a Golden Globe for her performance in *Doubt*. In 2009, she played the character of the world-famous chef, Julia Child, in *Julie and Julia*. She portrayed the British Prime Minister Margaret Thatcher in *The Iron Lady* in 2011.

Meryl Streep holds the record of 21 nominations at the Academy Awards. She has won three of them. She has also had 31 Golden Globe nominations and won nine times. The British Academy Film Awards have nominated her thirteen times and awarded her twice. She has also won two Screen Actors Guild Awards.

Streep has been honored with three Primetime Emmy Awards. She has also received a Tony Award. In 2004, she was honored with the American Film Institute's Lifetime Achievement

Award. In 2011, she received the Kennedy Center Honors. She received the National Medal of Freedom in 2014. Streep is also the National Spokesperson of the National Woman's History Museum.

Streep married the sculptor Don Gummer in 1978. They have four children together.

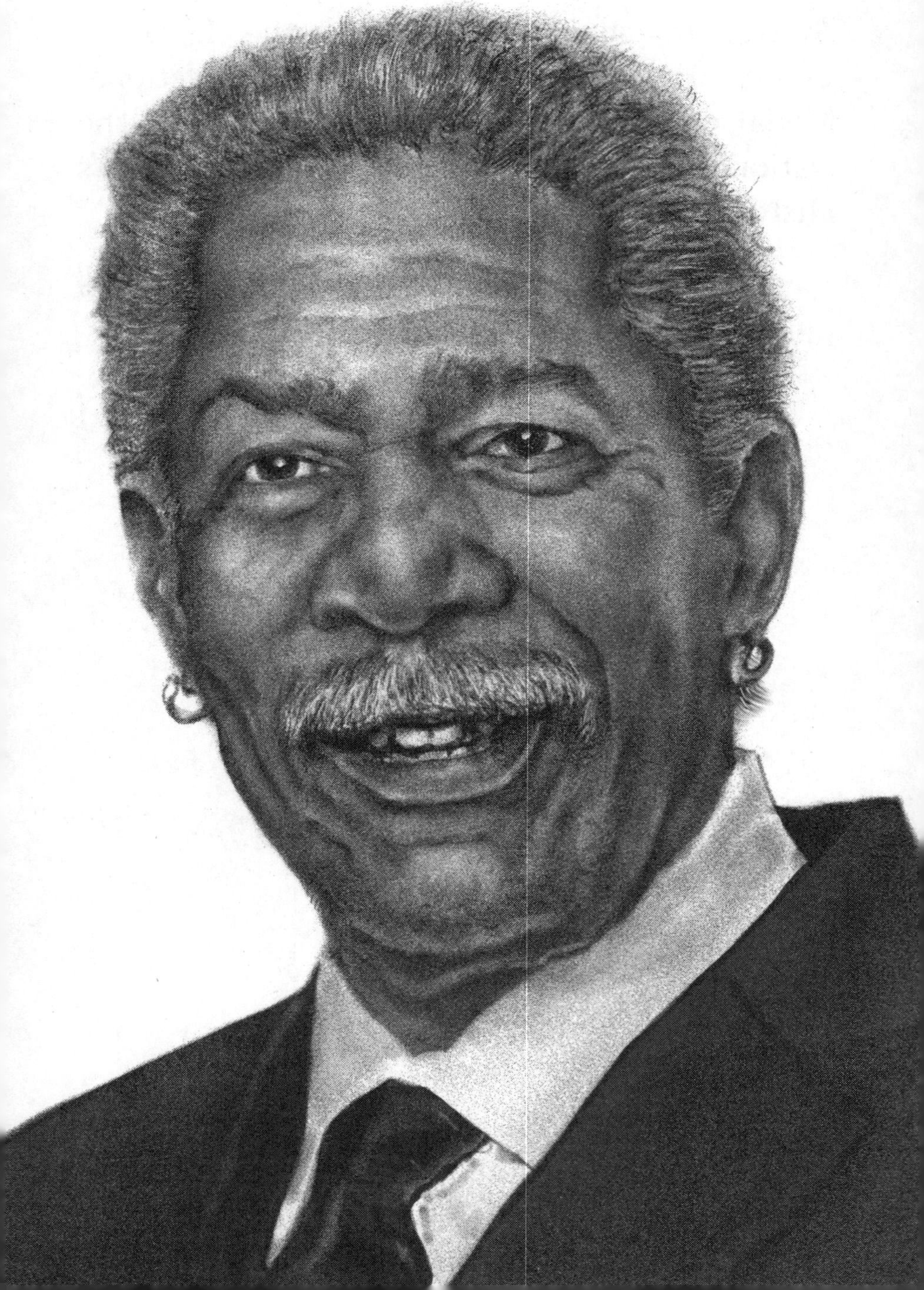

MORGAN FREEMAN

BIRTH: June 1, 1937
Tennessee, USA

Morgan Freeman is an American actor, narrator and producer. He is known for his remarkable roles in *The Shawshank Redemption, Glory, Driving Miss Daisy* and *The Dark Knight trilogy.*

Morgan Freeman was born on June 1, 1937 in Memphis, Tennessee. His mother, Mayme Edna, was a teacher. His father, Grafton Curtis was a barber.

In 1955, Freeman joined the US Air Force. He wanted to become a fighter pilot but had to work as a radar technician and mechanic instead. He finally left the Air Force in 1959 to pursue a career in acting.

Freeman took acting lessons at Los Angeles City College in the early 1960s. He joined the Opera Ring Musical Theatre Group. He made his Broadway debut in *Hello Dolly!* in 1967.

From 1971, Freeman started appearing on the television. He was part of the children's program *The Electric Company,* which ran for five years. He was nominated for a Tony award for his work in *The Mighty Gents* from 1978. He started his career in Hollywood with minor roles in films such as *Brubaker, Harry & Son* and *Marie.*

In 1987, Freeman bagged his first lead role in the film *Street Smart.* This role earned him an Academy Award nomination for the 'Best Supporting Actor'. His next performance in the comedy *Driving Miss Daisy* earned him a Golden

Globe and another Academy Award nomination. He starred in Zwick's *Glory* in 1989. It was based on the first recognized African-American units of the Civil War. Morgan was part of the 1994 *The Shawshank Redemption*, based on Stephen King's novel *Rita Hayworth and Shawshank Redemption*.

Freeman played the role of God in the 2003 comedy *Bruce Almighty* starring Jim Carrey. He also acted in its sequel *Evan Almighty*. In 2004, Freeman played the role of an elderly trainer, Eddie Dupris, in Clint Eastwood's *Million Dollar Baby*. His performance earned him an Academy Award for 'Best Supporting Actor'.

Freeman portrayed the South African president Nelson Mandela in *Invictus*, directed by Clint Eastwood. This was based on the events that took place in South Africa before and after the Rugby World Cup of 1995. This earned him another Academy Award nomination.

Freeman is known for his deep, resounding voice and hence, has lent it to action movies like *War of the Worlds* and animated movies like *The*

Lego Movie.

Freeman has been nominated six times for the Golden Globes and five times for the Academy Awards. He won a Screen Actors Guild Award for *Million Dollar Baby*. In 2006, Freeman was honored with the first ever Mississippi's Best Award. The American Film Institute gave him the Lifetime Achievement Award in 2012. He was awarded the Cecil B. DeMille Award by the Golden Globes for his contribution to cinema in 2012. President Barack Obama presented him with the 2015 National Medal of Arts. Freeman was the 54th recipient of the SAG (Screen Actors Guild) Life Achievement Award.

The movie production company Revelations Entertainment was co-founded by Freeman in 1996. He started the organization Rock River Foundation, contributing to many educational programs. He helped raise money for victims of hurricane Ivan in Grenada and hurricane Katrina. Freeman turned his ranch to a beekeeping sanctuary in 2014.

Morgan Freeman has been married twice. His last marriage was to Myrna Colley-Lee. They got divorced in 2010.

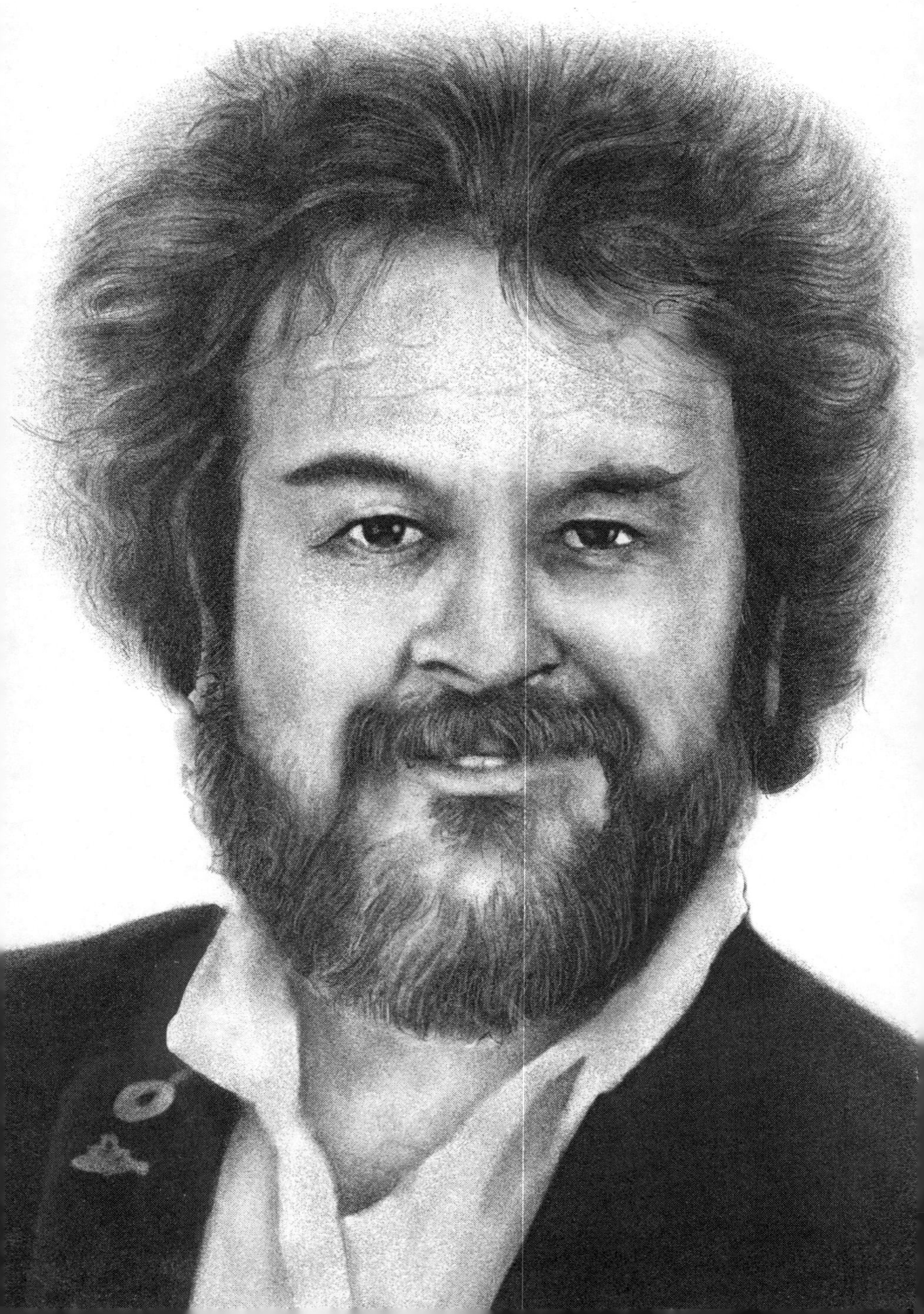

PETER JACKSON

BIRTH: *October 31, 1961*
North Island, New Zealand

Peter Jackson is a film director and screenwriter from New Zealand, wildly popular for his adaptation of JRR Tolkien's *The Lord of the Rings.*

Sir Peter Robert Jackson was born on October 31, 1961, in Pukerua bay, New Zealand. His parents were English immigrants. They gifted him an 8-mm camera to develop his interest in movies as a child. In 1969, he saw the original King Kong and was inspired to remake it.

He started working as a photograph lithographer for the local newspaper. He saved the money from this job to buy a state-of-the-art camera. After receiving a grant from the New Zealand Film Commission, he quit his job to film *Bad Taste*. The movie debuted at the Cannes film festival in 1987. It became an instant hit and got many distribution deals.

Jackson's *Meet the Feebles* was released in 1989. In 1992, Jackson's horror film *Braindead* (titled Dead Alive in the US) was released. It gained a cult status in this genre. It is also considered to be one of the goriest films ever made, and has won international awards in science fiction.

Jackson's 1994 release, *Heavenly Creatures*, received much commercial and critical appreciation. It was based on real-life events. This film gave Kate Winslet her first major role. It was part of the top ten films of the year. Next, he collaborated with Costa Botes to create the mockumentary, *Forgotten Silver*. In 1996, his first big-budget Hollywood film, *The Frighteners* was released.

Jackson ventured into his next project, which was adapting JRR Tolkien's *Lord of the Rings* for the big screen. He gained its rights and planned to release it as a trilogy. His project was financed by New Line Cinema. The first film of the series, *The Fellowship of the Ring*, was released in 2001. It gained international recognition and critical success; it won four Academy Awards. The second film, *The Two Towers*, was released in 2002. And the last film of the trilogy, *The Return of the King*, was released in 2003. It became one of the highest grossing films of all time. It won 11 of the 12 nominations it had received at the Academy Awards. It is ranked with Titanic and Ben-Hur for the most Academy Awards won by a single film.

Peter Jackson and Michael Stephens founded the production company WingNut Films in 2003. It has been involved in the creation of Jackson's films. Jackson's childhood dream was realized when he remade the 1933 classic, *King Kong* in

2005. It received three Academy Awards.

Peter Jackson took up the project of *The Hobbit,* a prequel to Tolkien's *The Lord of the Rings*. This was also created as a trilogy with films titled *The Hobbit: An Unexpected Journey, The Hobbit: The Desolation of Smaug* and *The Hobbit: The Battle of Five Armies*. They were released in 2012, 2013 and 2014 respectively.

Jackson has received three Academy Awards in his career so far. He won the Academy Award for 'Best Director' in 2004. He has been awarded a Golden Globe and four BAFTAs. He has received three Australian Film Institute Awards. He has won two Producer's Guild of America Awards and three New Zealand Film and TV Awards. Jackson was honored with a star at the Hollywood Walk of Fame in 2014. In 2002, Jackson was made a Knight Companion of the New Zealand Order of Merit.

He owns The Vintage Aviator, an aircraft manufacturing and restoration company. It is dedicated to the fighter planes of World War I and World War II. He has contributed towards accentuating stem cell research and the defense fund as well. Jackson married Fran Walsh, a screenwriter, in 1987. They have two children together. Walsh has co-written the scripts of *Heavenly Creatures* and *The Lovely Bones* with Jackson.

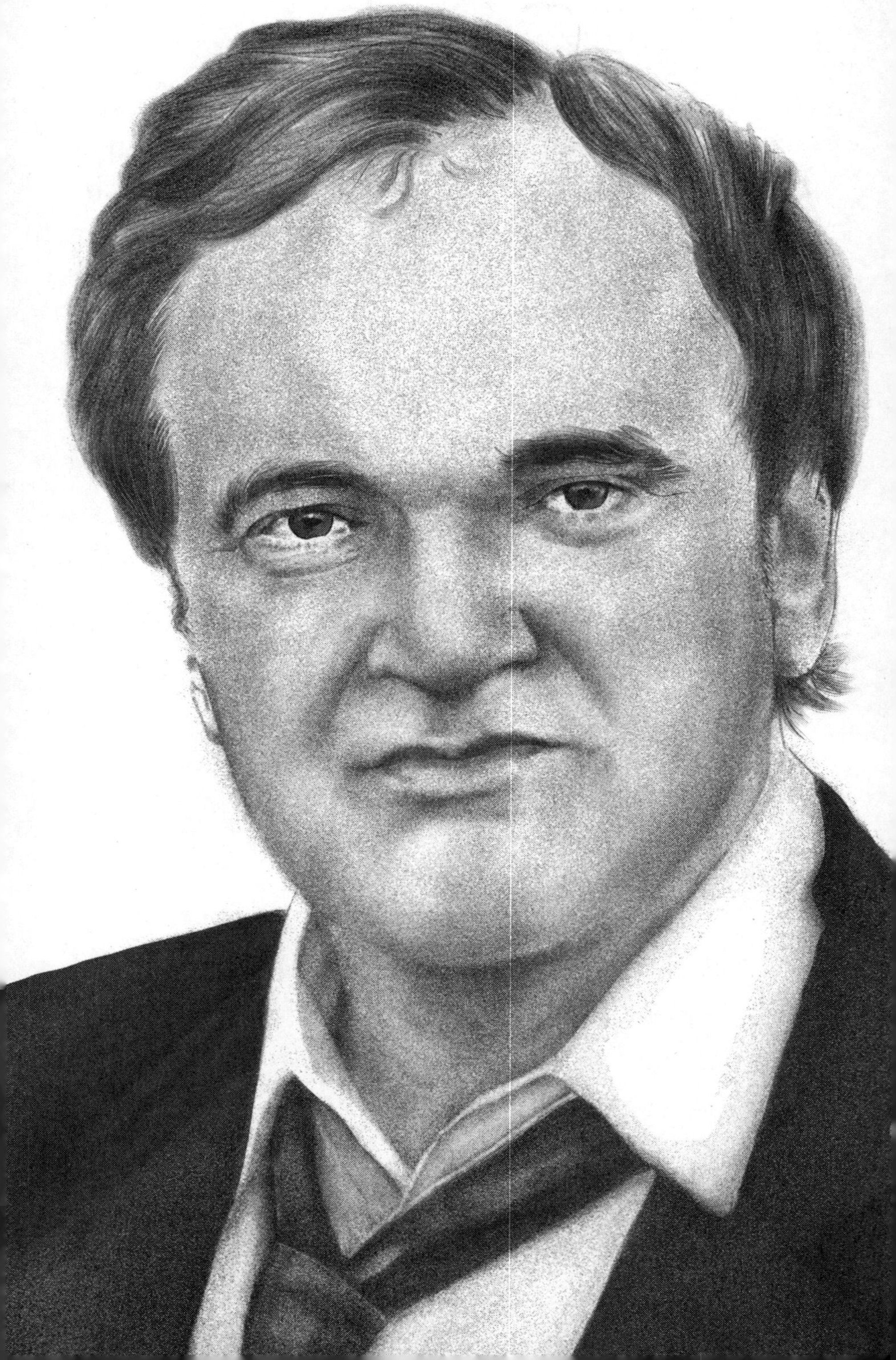

QUENTIN TARANTINO

BIRTH: *March 27, 1963*
Knoxville, Tennessee, USA

Quentin Tarantino is an American director, actor and screenwriter. He is known for delivering classics like *Pulp Fiction, Inglourious Basterds* and *Django Unchained.*

Quentin Jerome Tarantino was born in Knox- ville, Tennessee, on March 27, 1963. His father, Tony Tarantino, was an actor. His mother, Connie McHugh, was a nurse. Tarantino moved to California when he was four years old. His mother and stepfather, Curt Zastoupil, raised him.

Tarantino was raised in a middle-class family and started attending the James Best Theater Company for acting classes. He also worked as an usher at an adult film theater. In the 1980s, Tarantino worked at a video store, Video Archives, in Manhattan Beach, which eventually became more of film college for him. He worked there for five years.

He began his career by selling two screenplays which later became *True Romance* and *Oliver Stone's Natural Born Killers*. He made his directorial debut in 1992 with the film *Reservoir Dogs*, a movie on a failed jewelry robbery. Tarantino wrote and directed *Four Rooms* in 1995. He then wrote Robert Rodriguez's *From Dusk till Dawn* in 1996. The following year, he directed *Jackie Brown*, a blaxploitation film starring *Pam Grier*. It was based on Elmore Leonard's novel *Rum Punch*.

In 2003, Tarantino's *Kill Bill: Vol. 1* was released, with Uma Thurman as its star. Its sequel was released the next year, named *Kill Bill: Vol. 2*. He won various International award nominations for the same, along with European Film Awards. It was a film about a female assassin seeking revenge.

Tarantino presided over the Jury at the Cannes Film Festival in 2004. He even ventured into television at this point. He directed an episode of *CSI: Crime Scene Investigation* in 2005. It earned him a nomination at the Emmy Awards.

Tarantino collaborated with Director Roger Rodriguez in 2005 for Sin City. His 2007 collaboration with Rodriguez for Grindhouse was, however, not successful. Tarantino wrote and directed the 2009 film *Inglourious Basterds*. This movie, set during World War 2, is about the Jewish Americans who were trained to fight the Nazis in German-occupied France. It was a huge commercial hit starring Brad Pitt. It got nominated for eight Academy Awards and was showcased at the 62nd Cannes Film Festival.

In 2012, his movie *Django Unchained* was released. It was a Western, set in the antebellum American South, that gained both critical and commercial acclaim. The movie depicts the story of a free slave endeavoring to save his wife from a manor proprietor.

Tarantino was awarded the Palme d'Or at the Cannes film festival for Pulp Fiction in 1994. He received an Academy Award in the category 'Best Writing/Original Screenplay' in 1995. In 2010, Tarantino won a Critics Choice Award for 'Best Original Screenplay' for *Inglourious Basterds*. In 2011, he won the Honorary César award. In 2013, the Rome Film Festival honored him with the Lifetime Achievement Award.

Tarantino received an Academy Award for Django Unchained in 2013. In the same year, he won a BAFTA award in the category 'Best Original Screenplay'. He also won a Golden Globe for this movie. In the December of 2015, Tarantino was honored with a star on the Hollywood Walk of Fame. Quentin Tarantino's career "was a Hollywood dream story" according to Daniel Fierman from Entertainment Weekly.

Tarantino was in a long term relationship

with actress Mira Sorvino. He got married to the Israeli singer Daniela Pick in 2018. The couple welcomed a baby boy in February 2020.

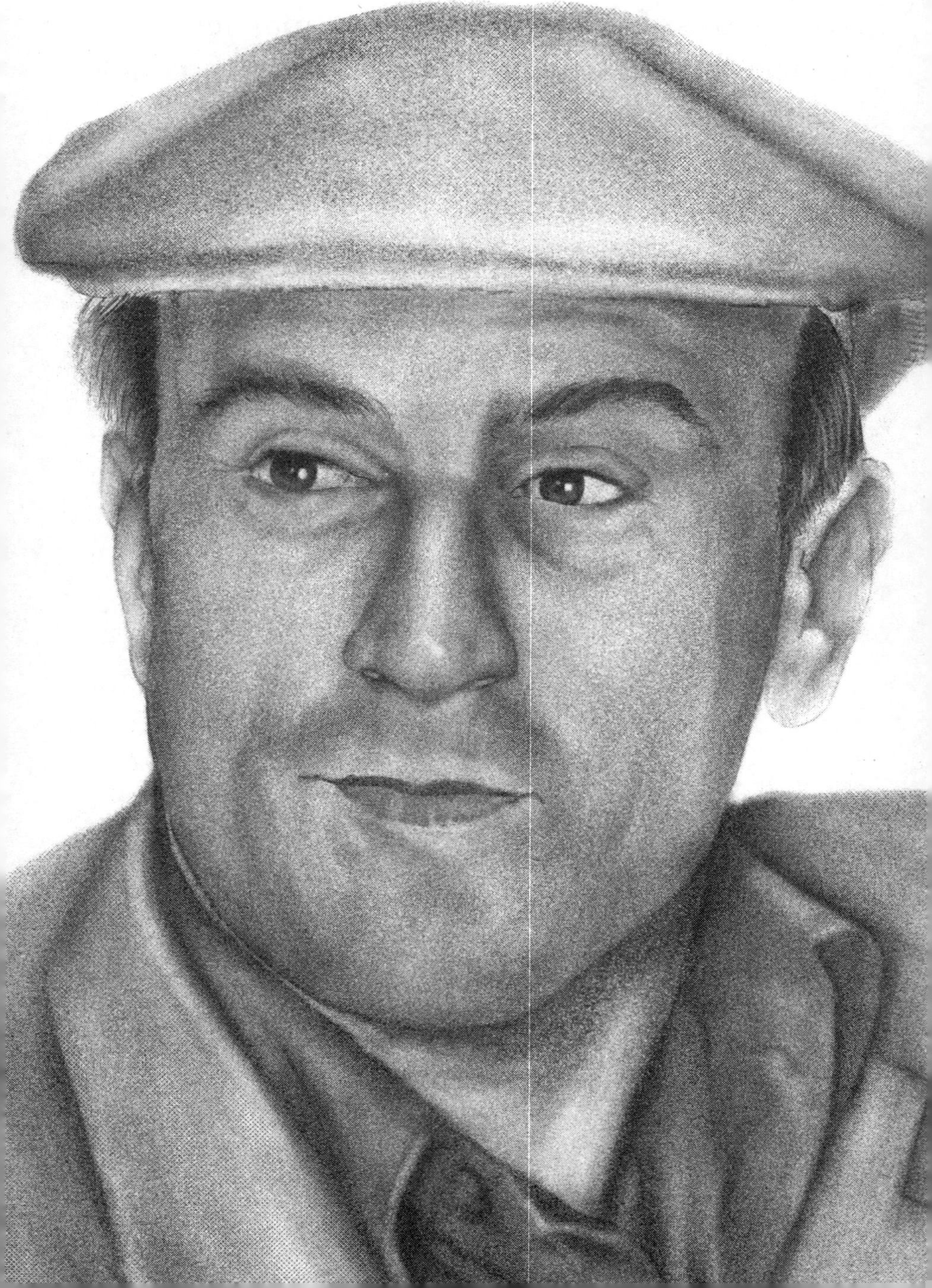

ROBERT DE NIRO

BIRTH: *August 17, 1943*
New York City, USA

Robert De Niro is an American actor, director and producer. He is widely appreciated for his work in movies such as *Awakenings, The Intern* and *Taxi Driver.*

Robert De Niro, Jr. was born on August 17, 1943 in Greenwich Village, New York. His father, Robert De Niro, Sr., was a sculptor and a painter. His mother, Virginia Holton Admiral, was a professional painter and poet. His parents got divorced when he was three years old and he was raised by his mother.

Robert dropped out of school to pursue a career in acting. He took acting classes from the Stella Adler Conservatory and Lee Strasberg's Actors Studio. De Niro's debut on-screen was with a minor role in *The Wedding Party* filmed in 1963 alongside Jill Clayburgh. He also had some cameos in French movies such as *Three Rooms* in Manhattan. His first lead role was in the movie *Greetings*, in 1968.

De Niro gained real recognition after his performance in the 1973 releases *Bang the Drum Slowly and Mean Streets*. His fame escalated after his portrayal of Vito Corleone in Coppola's *The Godfather: Part II,* in 1974. This role won him an Academy Award.

In 1976, De Niro acted in Bertolucci's *1900* and Elia Kazan's *The Last Tycoon*. He teamed up with Scorsese for *Raging Bull* in 1980. His role as Jake La Motta won him an Academy Award in 1981.

In the 1990s, he received admiration for his work in Scorsese's gangster movie *Goodfellas*.

In the movie *Awakenings*, De Niro portrayed a catatonic patient. His directorial debut took place with *A Bronx Tale* in 1993. In Kenneth Branagh's adaptation of Mary Shelley's classic Frankenstein, De Niro played the creature created by Frankenstein. He ended the decade with *Analyze This*. It was a spoof of mob movies and garnered commercial success.

De Niro started the next decade by acting in the American comedy *Meet the Parents* in 2000. This was followed by its sequels, *Meet the Fockers and Little Fockers*. In 2002, he hosted *9/11*, a CBS documentary on the attacks of September 11, 2001. His other movies from this decade include *Stardust and Everybody's Fine,* among others.

De Niro played Senator John McLaughlin in the directorial venture of Rodriguez and Ethan Maniquis, called *Machete*. He was also a part of the film adaptation of the novel *The Dark Fields* by Neil Burger called *Limitless*.

De Niro acted in David O. Russel's *Silver Linings Playbook* in 2012. This earned him an Academy nomination. In 2015, De Niro was again a part of Russel's cast for *Joy* starring Jennifer Lawrence and Bradley Cooper. He also starred in Nancy Meyer's *The Intern*, released in the same year. In 2016, he played Ray Arcel in the biopic *Hands of Stone*. De Niro played the role of Bernie Madoff in the HBO film *The Wizard of Lies*. He earned a Golden Globe nomination for his performance.

De Niro has been nominated eight times for Academy Awards, including in the category of 'Best Actor' for *Raging Bull* and 'Supporting Actor' in *The Godfather: Part II*. He has been nominated at the BAFTA and Golden Globe Awards several times as well, and won both for Raging Bull.

In 2003, De Niro received the AFI (American Film Institute) Lifetime Achievement Award. In 2007, he was awarded at the Berlin International Festival for *The Good Shepherd*. He was given the Kennedy Center Honors in 2009. He was awarded the Golden Globe Cecil B. DeMille Award in 2011. De Niro received the Presidential Medal of Freedom from President Barack Obama in 2016.

De Niro supports and contributes to various charitable organizations. He is part of the Advisory Committee of the FilmAid International.

De Niro has been married twice. He is presently married to Grace Hightower. They have been married since 1997. He is a father of six children. His daughter, Drena De Niro, is also an actor.

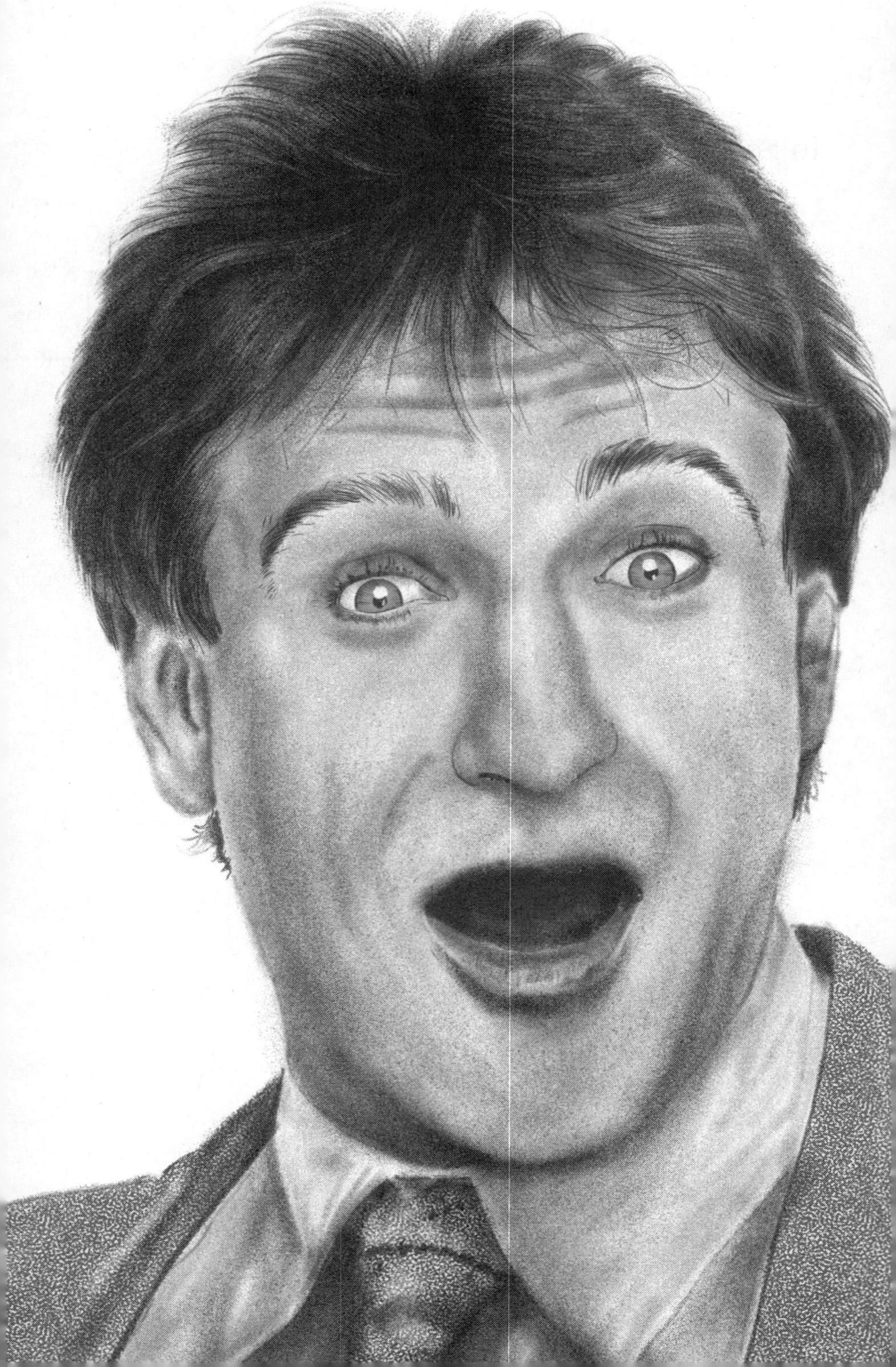

ROBIN WILLIAMS

BIRTH: July 21, 1951
Chicago, Illinois, USA

DEATH: August 11, 2014 (aged 63)
Paradise Cay, California, USA

Robin Williams was an American actor and comedian. He was born on July 21, 1951 in Chicago, Illinois. His father, Robert Williams, was an executive at Ford motors. His mother, Laurie McLaurin, was a model. In 1973, Williams got a full scholarship to the Juilliard School of acting.

In the 1970s, Williams used to perform

stand-up comedy at comedy clubs, which is how he got his first big break. Williams got a chance to appear in the revival of the show *Laugh-In,* along with *The Richard Pryor Show.*

In the following year, he appeared in the role of Mork, the Alien in *Happy Days.* Williams' character got his own series, *Mork & Mindy,* with Pam Dawber, in 1978. Robin Williams performed a live comedy show at Copacabana called *Reality... What a Concept,* in 1978. The recording of this show won a Grammy Award.

Williams debuted in cinema with the comedy *Can I Do It 'Till I Need Glasses?* in 1977. He played Popeye the Sailor Man in *Popeye* in 1980. He acted as a Russian musician, Vladimir Ivanoff, in *Moscow on the Hudson.* This earned him a nomination at the Golden Globe Awards.

In 1987, *Good Morning, Vietnam* was released, in which Williams played the role of a DJ at the radio station of the *Armed Forces.* He portrayed the character of an English teacher, John Keating, in *Dead Poets* Society in 1989. Williams received

Academy Award nominations for both movies.

Williams acted alongside Robert De Niro and Julie Kavner in Penny Marshall's *Awakenings*. He portrayed the character of a homeless man, Parry, in *The Fisher King*. He acted as Peter Banning in *Hook*, in 1991. He also gave voice to the genie in the animated movie *Aladdin* in 1992. Williams acted in several memorable movies in the 1990s such as *Mrs. Doubtfire*, *Jumanji* and *The Birdcage*. Williams played the role of a psychiatrist in *Good Will Hunting*. The movie gained immense popularity. His performance won him an Academy Award for 'Best Supporting Actor'.

In 2002, Williams played the character of a psychotic photo-developer in *One Hour Photo*. He played a writer of pulp novels in *Insomnia*. Williams portrayed former President Teddy Roosevelt in *Night at the Museum* in 2006. He starred alongside Mandy Moore and John Krasinski in the hilarious comedy License to Wed in 2007.

In 2009, Robin Williams performed his

stand-up comedy show called *Weapons of Self Destruction* in Washington, his first televised stand-up performance in seven years. He played Teddy Roosevelt once again in *Night at the Museum: Battle of the Smithsonian.*

Williams acted in the Broadway production of *Bengal Tiger* at the Baghdad Zoo in 2011. He was a voice actor in the animated movie *Happy Feet Two* the same year. He played Dwight D. Eisenhower in *The Butler* (2013). In the same year, he returned to television with the sitcom *The Crazy Ones.*

Williams received an Academy Award in the category of 'Best Supporting Actor' in 1998. He received seven Golden Globes. He has been awarded the Emmy Award twice and the Grammy Award four times.

In 1980, he was given a Grammy for 'Best Comedy Album' for *Reality... What a Concept.* In 19976 and 1998, he was honored with the Screen Actors Guild Award for *The Birdcage and Good Will Hunting.* In 2005, he was honored with the Golden Globe Cecil B. DeMille Award.

Williams was married twice and had three children. Despite being a positive influence and a source of laughter for many people through his career, Williams suffered from depression and anxiety in his personal life which led him to commit suicide. He died on August 11, 2014 at the age of 63.

Williams' movies *Merry Friggin' Christmas* and *Night at the Museum: Secret of the Tomb* were released posthumously.

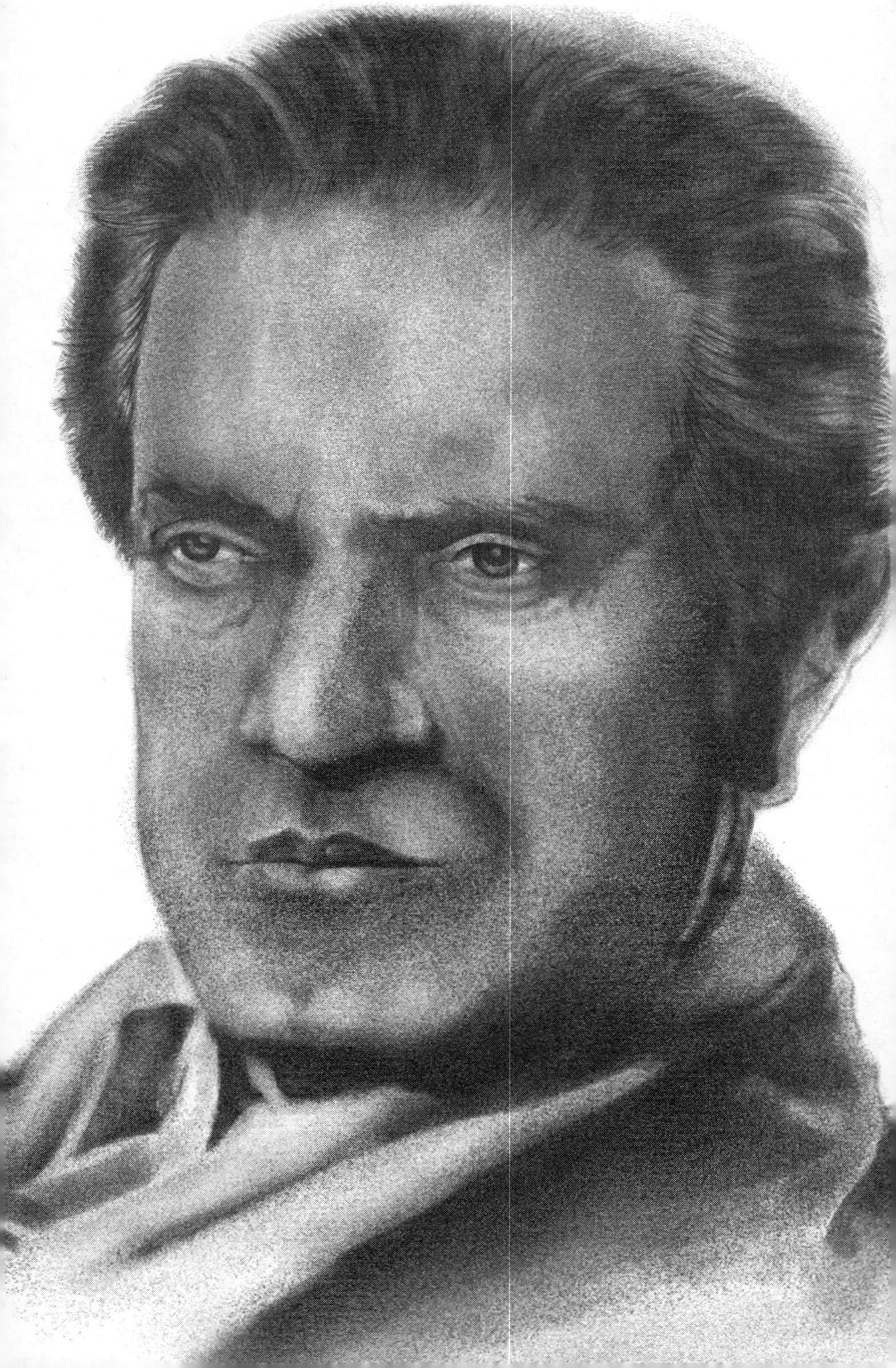

SATYAJIT RAY

BIRTH: May 2, 1921
Calcutta, Bengal Presidency, British India

DEATH: April 23, 1992 (aged 70)
Calcutta, West Bengal, India

Satyajit Ray was an Indian filmmaker, fiction writer, illustrator, publisher and calligrapher. He is known to have brought international recognition to Indian cinema, with movies like *Pather Panchali* and its sequels, together called the Apu trilogy.

Satyajit Ray was born on May 2, 1921 in Calcutta, India. He was the only child of his parents, Sukumar and Suprabha Ray. His father was a writer and illustrator. He came from an affluent Bengali family with rich cultural heritage. Ray attended the art school Visva-Bharati University in Shantiniketan. His interest in Indian art began here.

Ray started as a junior visualizer at a British advertising agency in 1943. He also worked for Signet Press, designing covers for books. During his time at the publishing press, Ray worked on *Pather Panchali*, a children's book by Bibhuti Bhushan Banerjee. This work also became the subject of his first film. Satyajit Ray founded the Calcutta Film Society along with Chidananda Dasgupta in 1947, where they would screen foreign films.

Ray was inspired to become a filmmaker by the French director Jean Renoir. The shooting for his first film *Pather Panchali* began in 1952. It was funded mostly by Ray himself with contributions from the West Bengal government. The shooting was completed by 1955 and the film released in the same year. It gained great commercial and critical response. It also won an award at the Cannes

International Film Festival in 1956.

This was followed by the other installments of the trilogy, *Aparajito (The Unvanquished) and Apur Sansar (The World of Apu)*. The films followed the protagonist, Apu, from childhood to maturity, coupled with a shift from village life to city life in Calcutta.

In 1961, Ray expanded the children's magazine, Sandesh, with Subhas Mukhopadhyay. He worked as an illustrator and writer for this magazine. His next project was *Charulata (The Lonely Wife)*. It was inspired by the works of Rabindranath Tagore, so were his other films, *Teen Kanya (Three Daughters)* and *Ghare Baire (The Home and the World)*.

Ray's musical fantasy *Goopy Gyne Bagha Byne (The Adventures of Gopi and Bagha)* became his most commercially successful film. It is based on a story by his grandfather. Ray also composed the songs for this film. Ray's 1962 film *Kanchenjungha* was his first film in color. It was also Ray's first original screenplay.

In 1977, Ray's first film in the Hindi language, *Shatranj Ke Khilari (The Chess Players)* was released. It explores the impact that the West had on India, showing the shift of power from ruler Wajid Ali to the British. In the 1970s, he created a trilogy of films titled *Pratidwandi (The Adversary)*, *Seemabaddha (Company Limited)* and *Jana Aranya (The Middleman)*. His 1989 *Ganashatru (An Enemy of the People)* is an adaptation of a play by Henrik Ibsen. In 1991, his last movie, *Agantuk (The Stranger)*, was released.

Satyajit Ray has been awarded 32 National Awards. He received two Silver Bears for 'Best Director' at the Berlin International Film Festival. He was also honored with a Golden Bear and a Golden Lion. He holds the record for the most Golden Bear nominations. He was a member of the Jury of Berlin International Festival in 1961. He was honored with 'Hommage à Satyajit Ray' at Cannes Film Festival in 1982.

Ray received an honorary doctorate from Oxford University in 1978. In 1985, he received the Dadasaheb Phalke Award. He was honored with the Legion of Honor by the President of France.

In 1992, Ray received an Academy Honorary Award. He received the Bharat Ratna, India's highest civilian award, from the Government of India in the same year. The Satyajit Ray Film and Television Institute was founded in 1995 under his name. The Satyajit Ray Award was created in his honor by the London Film Festival.

Satyajit Ray married Bijoya Das in 1949. They had a son, who also became a filmmaker. Ray passed away on April 23, 1992, due to a heart complication.

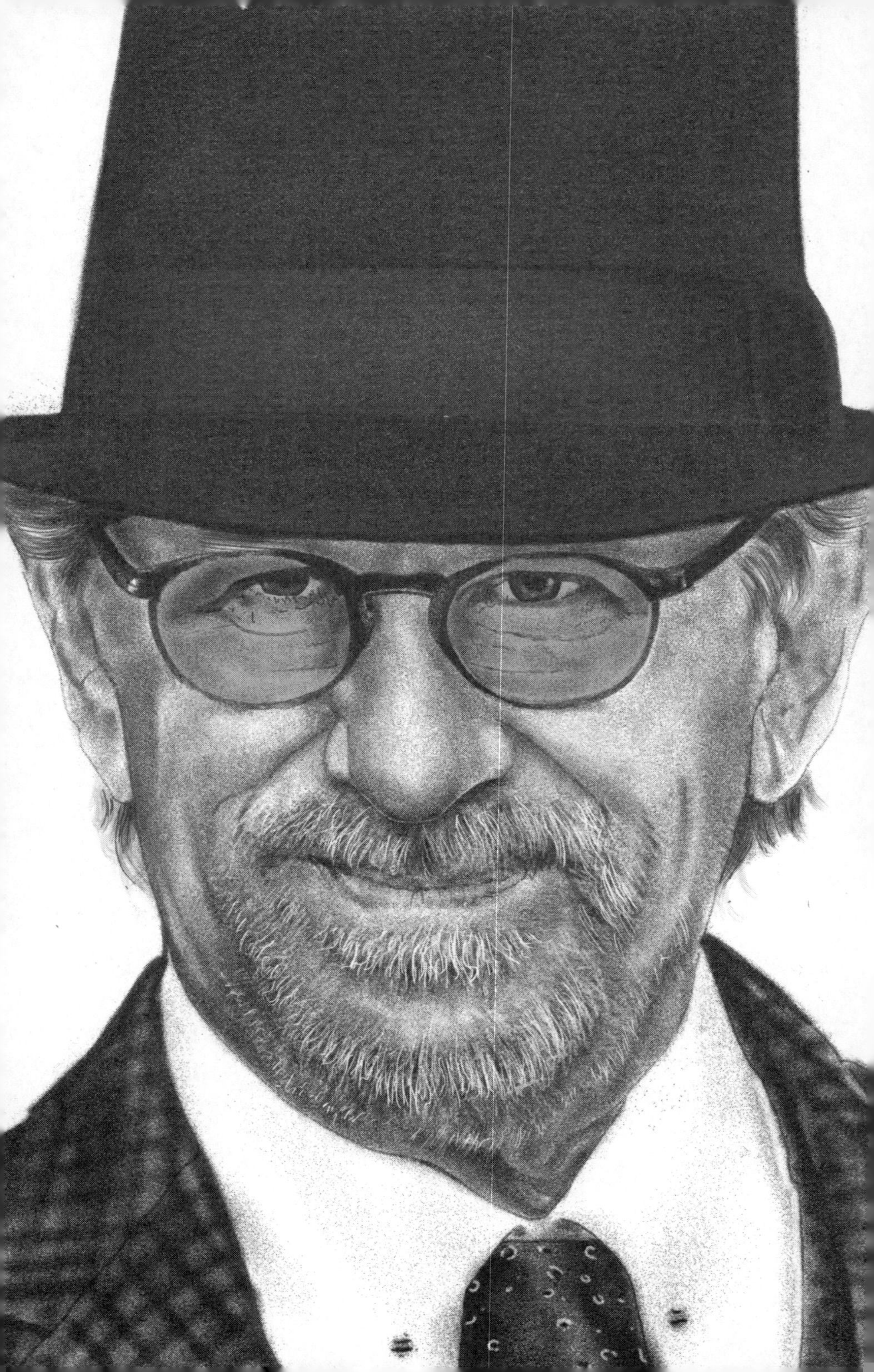

STEVEN SPIELBERG

BIRTH: *December 18, 1946*
Cincinnati, Ohio, USA

Steven Spielberg is an American director, producer and script-writer. He directs movies in various genres, including science fiction and historical fiction. He has worked as a movie-maker in Hollywood for more than four decades.

Steven Allan Spielberg was born to Leah Adler and Arnold Spielberg on December 18, 1946. He was raised in an Orthodox Jewish family.

In 1959, Spielberg created his first film, a

nine-minute movie called *The Last Gunfight*. He received a photography merit badge for this. He created a forty-minute war film, *Escape to Nowhere* when he was thirteen years old. It won the first prize at a film festival.

Spielberg produced his short film *Amblin'* in 1968. It won him many accolades and a seven-year contract with Universal Studios. As a professional, he started by directing several episodes of a television series filmed for Universal Studios. He has also directed segments in shows such as *Marcus Welby, M.D. and Columbo*. His 1971 television film, *Duel,* got him a contract to direct films with Universal. His next movie, *The Sugarland Express,* received critical acclaim.

Spielberg earned his reputation with his 1975 film, *Jaws.* It earned millions in its very first month. It gained popularity with the critics and the audience alike. His next project was a science fiction film called *Close Encounters of the Third Kind.*

In the 1980s, Spielberg's Indiana Jones

trilogy, *E.T.: The Extra-Terrestrial,* and *The Color Purple* were released. Spielberg founded Amblin Entertainment in 1981. He also founded the film studio DreamWorks SKG in 1994.

In 1991, he directed *Hook* inspired by Peter Pan. Spielberg's 1993 *Jurassic Park* was a box-office hit, and is still popular till date. Its sequel, called *The Lost World: Jurassic Park*, was released in 1997.

Spielberg shifted from adventure to drama with his 1993 film, *Schindler's List*. It won the Academy Award for 'Best Picture' in 1993 and Spielberg won 'Best Director'. In 1998, his movie, *Saving Private Ryan* was released. It became the biggest American film of the year.

His 2005 film, *War of the Worlds,* was a commercial success. Spielberg's Lincoln from 2012 got nominated for twelve Academy Awards. His 2015 movie, *Bridge of Spies,* starring Tom Hanks received six Academy Award nominations. In the following year, Spielberg directed the animated movie, *The*

BFG. In 2017, Spielberg's *The Post* was released. It got nominated at the Golden Globes and the Academy Awards.

The Academy of Motion Picture Arts and Sciences honored Spielberg with the Irving G. Thalberg Memorial Award in 1986. He received an honorary doctorate from the University of Southern California in 1994. Spielberg was awarded the Academy Award for 'Best Director' for his movie, *Saving Private Ryan.* In 2000, he received the Directors Guild of America Lifetime Achievement Award. He got inducted to the Science Fiction Hall of Fame in 2005. President Barack Obama awarded him the Presidential Medal of Freedom in 2015.

Spielberg established the Righteous Person Foundation with his earnings from *Schindler's List.* It funded projects to enhance the modern Jewish lifestyle. In 1991, he founded Starbright. It works towards improving the quality of life for children with chronic diseases. He also established the USC Shoah Foundation in 1994. It is dedicated to preserving the testimonies of the survivors of the Holocaust.

Spielberg has been married twice. His first marriage was to actor Amy Irving. They had a son together. His present wife is Kate Capshaw. They got married in 1991. Spielberg is a father of seven children.

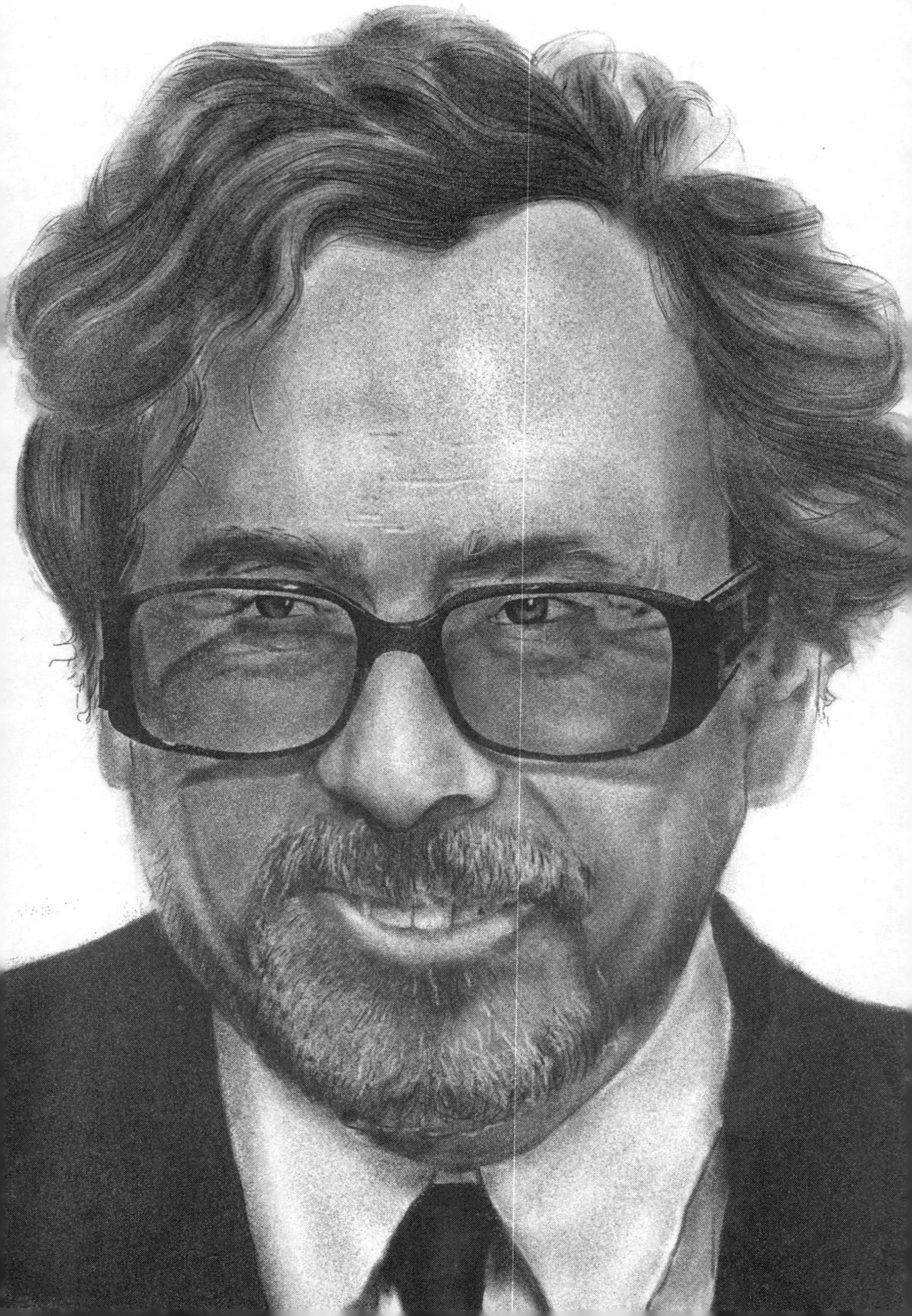

TIM BURTON

BIRTH: August 25, 1958
Burbank, California, USA

Tim Burton is an American filmmaker, producer, writer and animator. He is known for his dark horror and fantasy movies. His most successful films include *Batman, Edward Scissorhands, Planet of the Apes* and *Charlie and the Chocolate Factory*.

Tim Burton was born in the city of Burbank, California on August 25, 1958. His mother, Jean Burton, was the owner of a gift shop. His father, Bill Burton, was a former baseball player who worked at the Burbank Park.

Burton attended the California Institute for the Arts. He started creating short films at a very young age. He created *The Island of Doctor Agnor* when he was merely thirteen years old. Burton took up a course in character animation at the California Institute of Arts. He created *Stalk of the Celery Monster* and *King and the Octopus* during this time. He completed his education in 1979.

After graduating from the institute, Burton started working as an animator at Walt Disney Studios. He embarked upon his solo career after a year of working there. It was recognized at the Chicago Film Festival. Burton's 1984 *Frankenweenie* gave a new twist to the classic Frankenstein.

The success of these short films earned him a commission from Paul Reubens to direct Peewee's *Big Adventure*. It was his first collaboration with musician Danny Elfman. His next directorial venture, *Beetlejuice,* was released in 1988. Burton came to be known for his blend of horror and fantasy after this movie. His 1989 release, *Batman*, was a huge box office success.

Burton's next project, *Edward Scissorhands*, starred A-listers Johnny Depp and Winona Ryder. It was a love story with elements of social satire. It is considered to be one of his best movies. In 1992, the sequel to Batman was released, named *Batman Returns.*

Burton wrote and produced *The Nightmare Before Christmas*, an animated musical, in 1993. He released Ed Wood in 1994. He produced *Batman Forever* in 1995. It was directed by Joel Schumacher. After producing the animated production James and the Giant Peach, Burton directed the sci-fi movie *Mars Attacks!* He also directed *Sleepy Hollow* in 1999.

In 2001, Burton's *Planet of the Apes* was released and it was a huge commercial success. His 2003 fantasy *Big Fish* earned an Academy Award nomination and four Golden Globe nominations. Burton's *Charlie and the Chocolate Factory* starring Johnny Depp was released in 2005. It was nominated in the 'Costume Design' category at the Academy Awards. He also directed *Corpse Bride*, released in 2005. It was nominated at the Academy Awards and won the Saturn Award for 'Best Animated Film'.

In 2007, his musical *Sweeney Todd: The Demon Barber of Fleet Street* was released. The cast included Johnny Depp and Helena Bonham Carter. It gained much critical acclaim. Depp and Carter reunited for Burton's *Alice In Wonderland* in 2010. This was followed by *Dark Shadows*. Burton remade his 1984 short film, *Frankenweenie*, into a stop-motion film in 2012.

Burton directed *Big Eyes* in 2014, based on the life of the artist Margaret Keane. His 2016 project was a fantasy film named *Miss Peregrine's Home for Peculiar Children*. It was based on a novel by Ransom Riggs.

Burton was awarded the Golden Lion for Lifetime Achievement in 2007. In 2010, Burton served as the President of the Jury of the 63rd Cannes Film Festival.

Burton is also a writer, with books like *Burton on Burton* and *The Melancholy Death of Oyster Boy and Other Stories* to his credit. *The Art of Tim*

Burton was written by Leah Gallo in 2009. Aside from being a writer and a filmmaker, Burton's drawings have been exhibited at New York City's Museum of Modern Art.

Burton married Lena Gieseke in 1989 but they divorced in 1991. He was then in a relationship with actor Helena Bonham Carter for thirteen years. They have one son together.

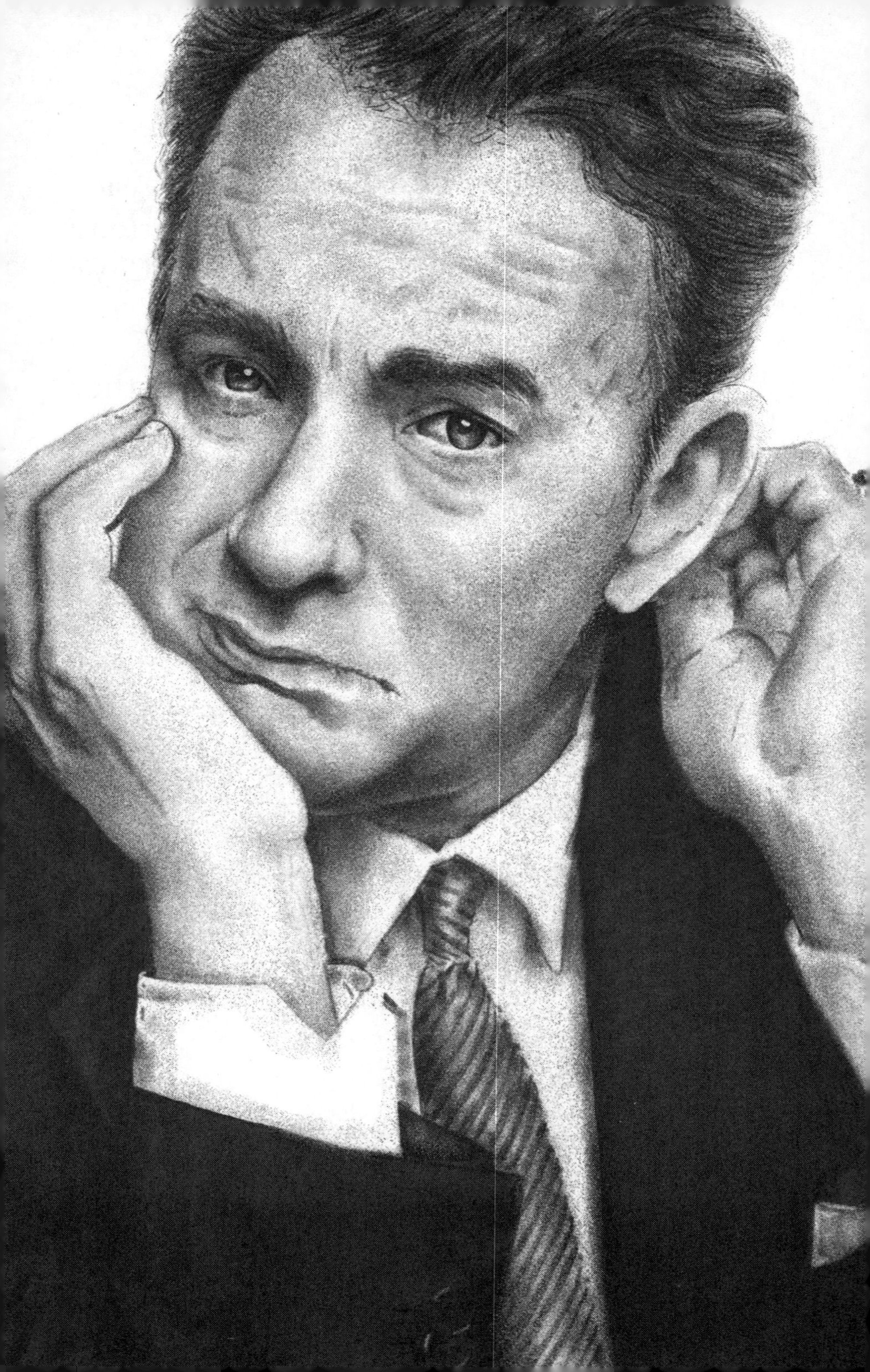

TOM HANKS

BIRTH: *July 9, 1956*
Concord, California, USA

Tom Hanks is an American actor and director. He is widely acclaimed for his roles in *Big, Forrest Gump* and *Cast Away*.

Tom Hanks was born Thomas Jeffrey Hanks on July 9, 1956, in California to Amos Mefford and Janet Marylyn. His parents divorced when he was only 5 and he, along with his two brothers, was raised solely by his father.

Hanks studied acting from the California State University. He dropped out of University in 1977 and took up an internship at the Great Lakes Shakespeare Festival. Hanks played the role of Proteus in Shakespeare's *Two Gentlemen of Verona* at the Great Lakes Theater Festival in 1978. It won him the 'Best Actor' Award from the Cleveland Critics Circle. Till 1980, he acted in various Shakespearean plays, while also working at a theater company in Sacramento.

Hanks moved to New York in the late 1970s. He made his on-screen debut with the horror movie *He Knows You're Alone.* He got recognition with the television series *Bosom Buddies.* In 1984, he acted in the hit comedy movie, *Splash.* He gave another blockbuster hit with Penny Marshal's *Big* in 1988. For this role, he had to act like a 13-year-old trapped in the body of a 35-year-old man.

Hanks won the Los Angeles Film Critic Award with his 1988 performance in *Big.* His role in Jonathan Demme's *Philadelphia* won him an Academy Award and an MTV Movie Award. He starred in the classic comedy-drama *Forrest Gump* in 1994. It won him another Academy Award. Hanks starred in Steven Spielberg's *Saving Private Ryan* in 1998. He then acted in the celebrated 1998 romantic-comedy *You've Got Mail* along with Meg Ryan.

Hanks gave voice to "Woody" in the animated movie series *Toy Story*. One of his most remarkable performances was in Zemeckis' *Cast Away*. Hanks got another Academy Award nomination for this role. He produced *My Big Fat Greek Wedding* in 2002 starring Nia Vardalos. In 2004, Hanks acted in Spielberg's *The Terminal* and Zemeckis' *The Polar Express*.

Hanks is perhaps most famous for playing Robert Langdon in Ron Howard's film adaptation of Dan Brown's novel *Da Vinci Code*. He also acted in its sequel, *Angels and Demons*, in 2009. In 2012, he starred in *Extremely Loud and Incredibly Close* and *Cloud Atlas*. He has also worked as an executive producer with Spielberg for the HBO series *The Pacific*. Hanks acted in the 2013 Broadway production of *Lucky Guy*. He got a Tony Award nomination for this role. In the same year, Hanks played Walt Disney in *Saving Mr. Banks*.

Hanks is the fourth-highest grossing actor in North America. He has earned two Academy Awards for *Philadelphia and Forrest Gump.* He and Spencer Tracy are the only two actors to have won Academy Awards for 'Best Actor' for two consecutive years. He has been awarded eight Golden Globes as well. He also received a Screen Actors Guild Award for *Forrest Gump.*

Hanks received a Lifetime Achievement Award from the American Film Institute in 2002. He received the Stanley Kubrick Britannia Award for Excellence in Film at the BAFTA Awards in 2004. He has been inducted to the United States Army Rangers Hall of Fame. Hanks received the Kennedy Center Honors in 2014. President Barack Obama presented him with the Presidential Medal of Freedom in 2016. He has also received the French Legion of Honor.

Hanks is involved in philanthropic and charitable ventures as well. He has contributed to the children's charity Elevate Hope Foundation. He also supports the Hole in the Wall Foundation. He has also served on the Board of Governors for the National Space Society. He is involved with a nonprofit called Surfrider Foundation, which cleans beaches.

Tom Hanks has been married twice. He is presently married to actor Rita Wilson. He is a father of four children. His son, Colin Hanks, is also an actor.

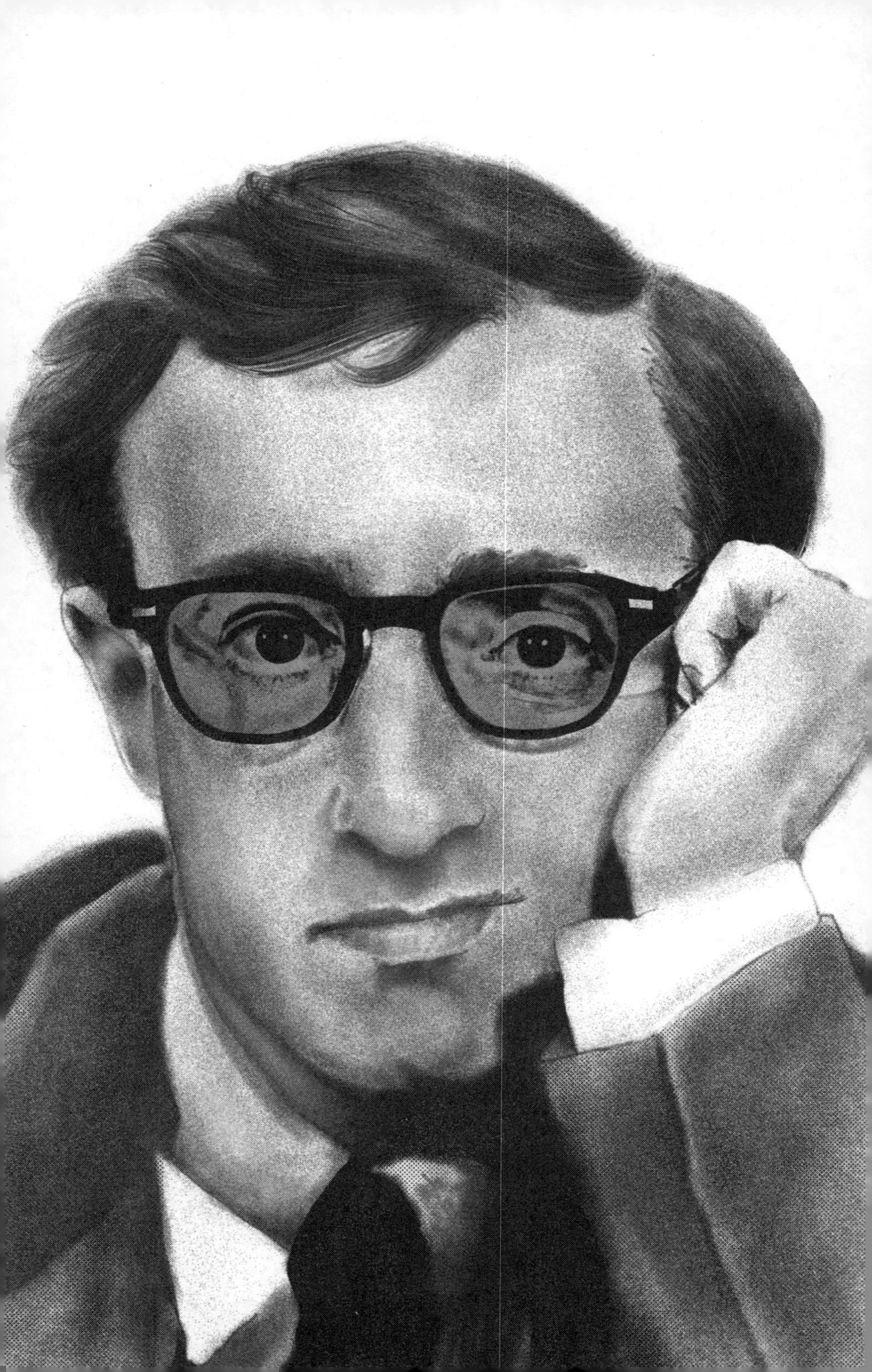

WOODY ALLEN

BIRTH: *December 1, 1935*
New York City, USA

Heywood "Woody" Allen is an American filmmaker, screenwriter, actor and comedian. He has had a career spanning over six decades. He is best known for directing and acting in Annie Hall and Manhattan.

Woody Allen was born as Allen Stewart Konigsberg on December 1, 1935 in New York City, to Nettie and Martin Konigsberg. His parents were second generation Jewish immigrants. Allen legally changed his name to

Heywood Allen when he was seventeen years old, after he was bullied at summer camp for being of a different race and ethnicity. Allen attended New York University for his higher education. He had poor attendance and poor grades and finally dropped out of school to begin writing scripts for television.

In 1954, he was assisting Sid Caesar to create scripts for shows such as *Sid Caesar's Chevy Show, Ed Sullivan Show* and *Your Show of Shows.* His work even earned him an Emmy nomination. In 1961, Allen debuted as a stand-up comedian at various clubs in Greenwich Village. He created a nervous, intellectual character for his comic routine.

Allen then took up playwriting. The 1965 comedy *What's New, Pussycat?* was his first produced screenplay. He made his Broadway debut with *Don't Drink the Water.*

Allen made his directorial debut with *What's Up, Tiger Lily?* in 1966. Mickey Rose assisted Allen for this movie. After this, Allen directed, wrote and starred in his own movies. His career flourished with *Take the Money and Run*, released in 1969. His following releases included *Play it Again, Sam and Sleeper.*

Allen's Annie Hall was released in 1977. He directed, starred in and co-wrote it with Marshall Brickman. It won four Academy Awards in the categories of 'Best Picture', 'Best Direction', 'Best Screenplay' and a 'Best Actress' award for Diane Keaton. His 1979 release Manhattan also earned him much critical and commercial acclaim. It was his homage to the city of New York.

In the 1980s, his movies *Stardust Memories* and *The Purple Rose of Cairo* were released. Allen won his second Academy Award for *Hannah and Her Sisters,* released in 1986. Towards the end of the 1990s, Allen's *Deconstructing Harry and Celebrity* were released. Both were dark satirical comedies.

Allen's next notable release was *Match Point* in 2005. The film had a box office collection of millions internationally. He also directed *Vicky*

Cristina Barcelona and *Midnight in Paris*. Allen was given the Academy Award for 'Best Original Screenplay' for *Midnight in Paris*. This movie is considered to be his most successful one. It has earned Golden Globes and Academy Awards. He appeared on screen after six years in *To Rome with Love*, in 2012.

So far, Woody Allen has received four Academy Awards and eleven BAFTA Awards in his career. He has also been honored with the BAFTA Fellowship. He has even won two Golden Globe awards and the Golden Globe Cecil B. Demille Award.

The screenplay of *Annie Hall* is ranked as the funniest screenplay by the Writers Guild of America. Allen has been awarded the Cesar Award for 'Best Foreign Film' for *Manhattan* and *The Purple Rose of Cairo*.

Allen is also well-appreciated for his comic monologues. Allen has a passion for jazz music as well. He has also played with his New Orleans Jazz Band in various hotels.

Woody Allen

Allen used to write humorous pieces which were published in the New York Times. PBS co-produced the biography *Woody Allen: A Documentary,* as part of the American Masters series in 2011. It was directed by Robert B. Weide.

Allen has been married three times. He is presently married to Soon Yi Previn. He is the father of six children.

QUESTIONS

Q.1.   What was Kurosawa's film Rashomon about and when was it released?

Q.2.   Which award did Al Pacino receive for his film *Scent of a Woman*?

Q.3.   In which movies did Katharine Hepburn show her remarkable performance?

Q.4.   What is the full name of Al Pacino?

Q.5.   Name a few movies directed by Alfred Hitchcock.

Q.6.   Who directed and acted in the comedy *A King in New York*? What was it about?

Q.7.   What was the name of the Broadway play that starred both Audrey Hepburn and Mel Ferrer?

Q.8.   When was Charlie Chaplin born and who were his parents?

Q.9.   Who was Akira Kurosawa?

Q.10. What was Alfred Hitchcock's first job?

Q.11. Which are the highest grossing films of Christopher Nolan?

Q.12. Where did Christopher Nolan receive his college education? What movies did he create in his college days?

Q.13. Mention Audrey Hepburn's achievements and awards.

Q.14. What was Clint Eastwood's first role with the Universal Studios?

Q.15. How many Academy awards did Daniel Day-Lewis receive for 'Best Actor'?

Q.16. Which are Johnny Depp's memorable movies?

Q.17. Where did Daniel Day-Lewis study acting?

Q.18. Who is the most nominated male actor in the Academy Awards' history?

Q.19. Leonardo DiCaprio starred in *Titanic* with Kate Winslet. Which other movies did they do together?

Q.20. Explain what The Vintage Aviator is and who created it.

Q.21. Which are Jack Nicholson's most celebrated films?

Q.22. Who is Quentin Tarantino and when was he born?

Q.23. Which year was Robin Williams born in?

Q.24. In which film did Robert De Niro play the character Travis Bickle?

Q.25. What is the name of Leonardo DiCaprio's production company?

Q.26. Who voiced the genie in Disney's *Aladdin*?

Q.27. For which movies is Meryl Streep best known?

Q.28. What is the highest honor that Satyajit Ray ever received?

Q.29. In which year was Steven Spielberg born?

Q.30. Who directed *The Lord of the Rings*?

DID YOU KNOW?

1. Over the years, Al Pacino has turned down many notable film roles, which went on to become iconic cinematic characters, such as Han Solo in *Star Wars*, and Ted Kramer in *Kramer vs Kramer*.

2. Robert De Niro uses a few choice acting techniques for his roles. He spends tons of time studying their backgrounds in detail.

3. Leonardo DiCaprio is one of the many celebrities who has signed with Virgin Galactic for a trip to space.

4. Robin Williams was initially offered the role of the Riddler in *Batman Forever*.

5. *The Dark Knight Rises* is Christopher Nolan's highest-grossing film in terms of worldwide earnings.

6. Morgan Freeman's first big break came in 1967 when he joined the production of *Hello, Dolly!* a musical.

7. Pacino worked with people from a school for the blind when he was doing *the Scent of a Woman*.

8. In 2001, Disney approached Tim Burton for a CGI sequel to *The Nightmare before Christmas*. However, Burton declined.

9. One of Meryl Streep's ancestors is William Penn, who founded the whole state of Pennsylvania.

10. Morgan Freeman, at the age of 78, received a Chaplin Award for his lasting commitment to cinema.

11. Clint Eastwood worked as a lumberjack, a forest firefighter, and a steelworker after he finished high school.

12. Meryl Streep is known for her mastery of accents and languages. Her Polish in *Sophie's Choice* was loved even by native speakers.

13. Eastwood tried to enroll into Seattle University but could not complete the process because he was drafted in the United States Army for the Korean War.

14. In 2017, Christopher Nolan received his first ever 'Best Director' nomination at the Oscars.